CAT MANDALAS

COLORING BOOKS FOR ADULTS

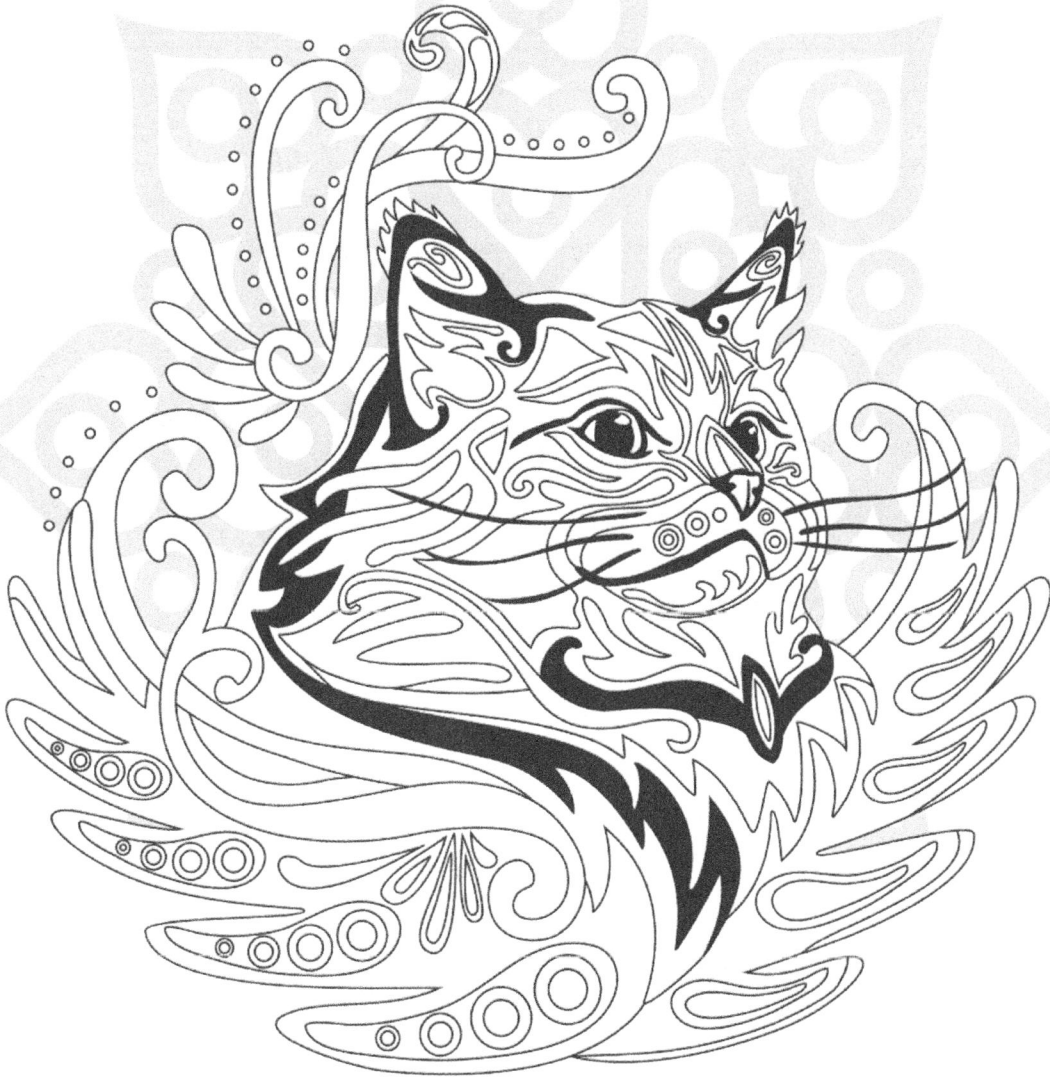

DAWN SHALHOUT

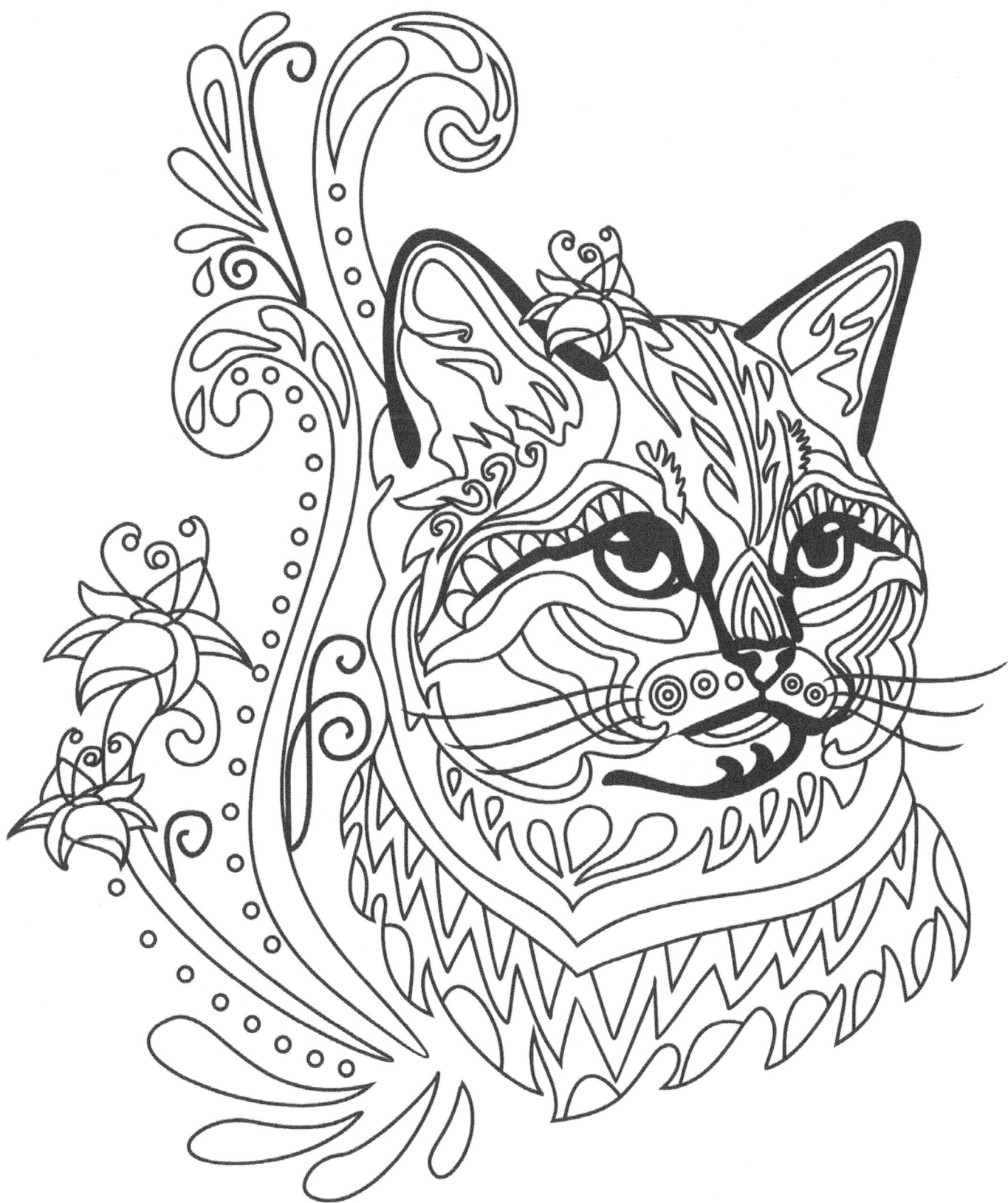

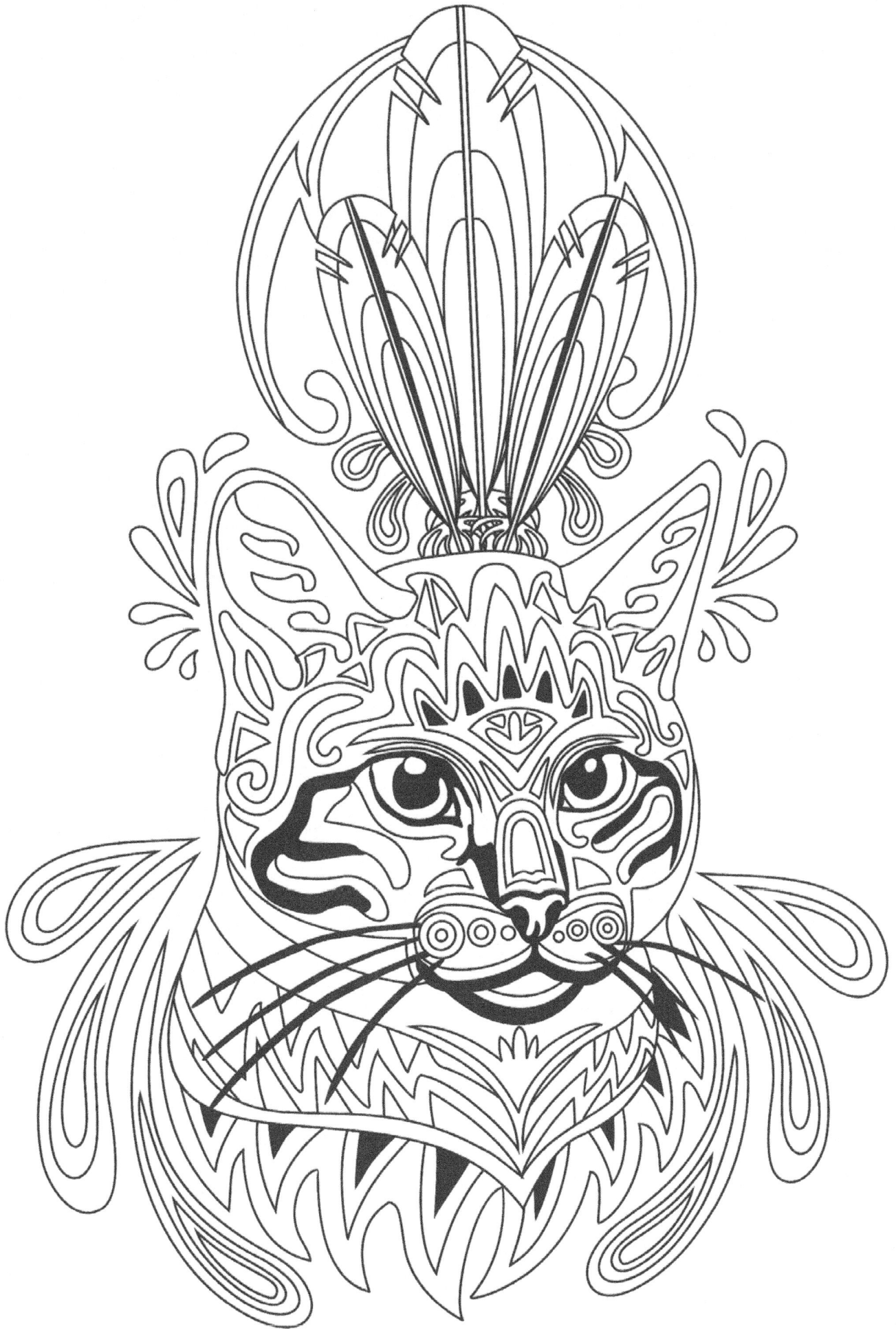

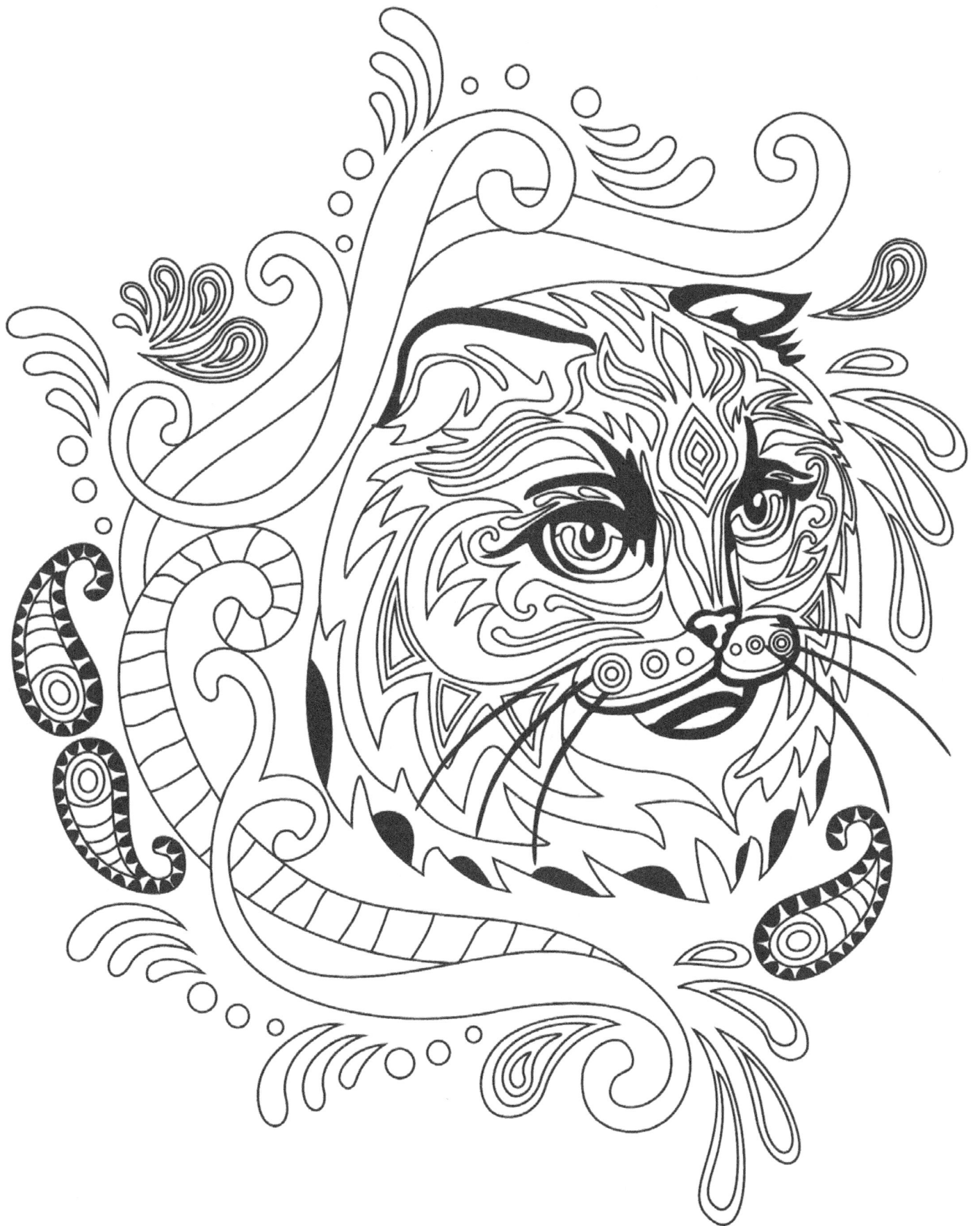

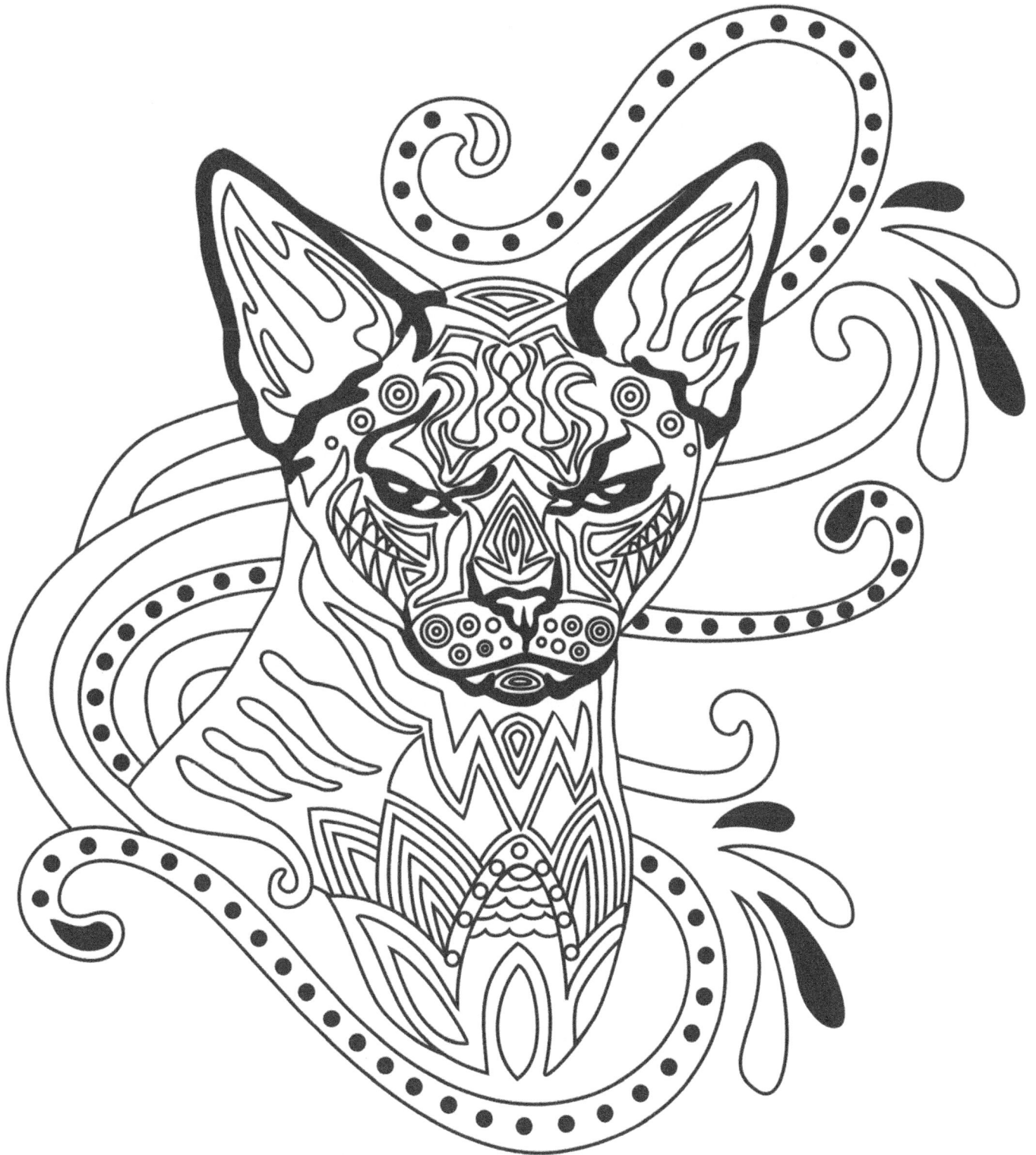

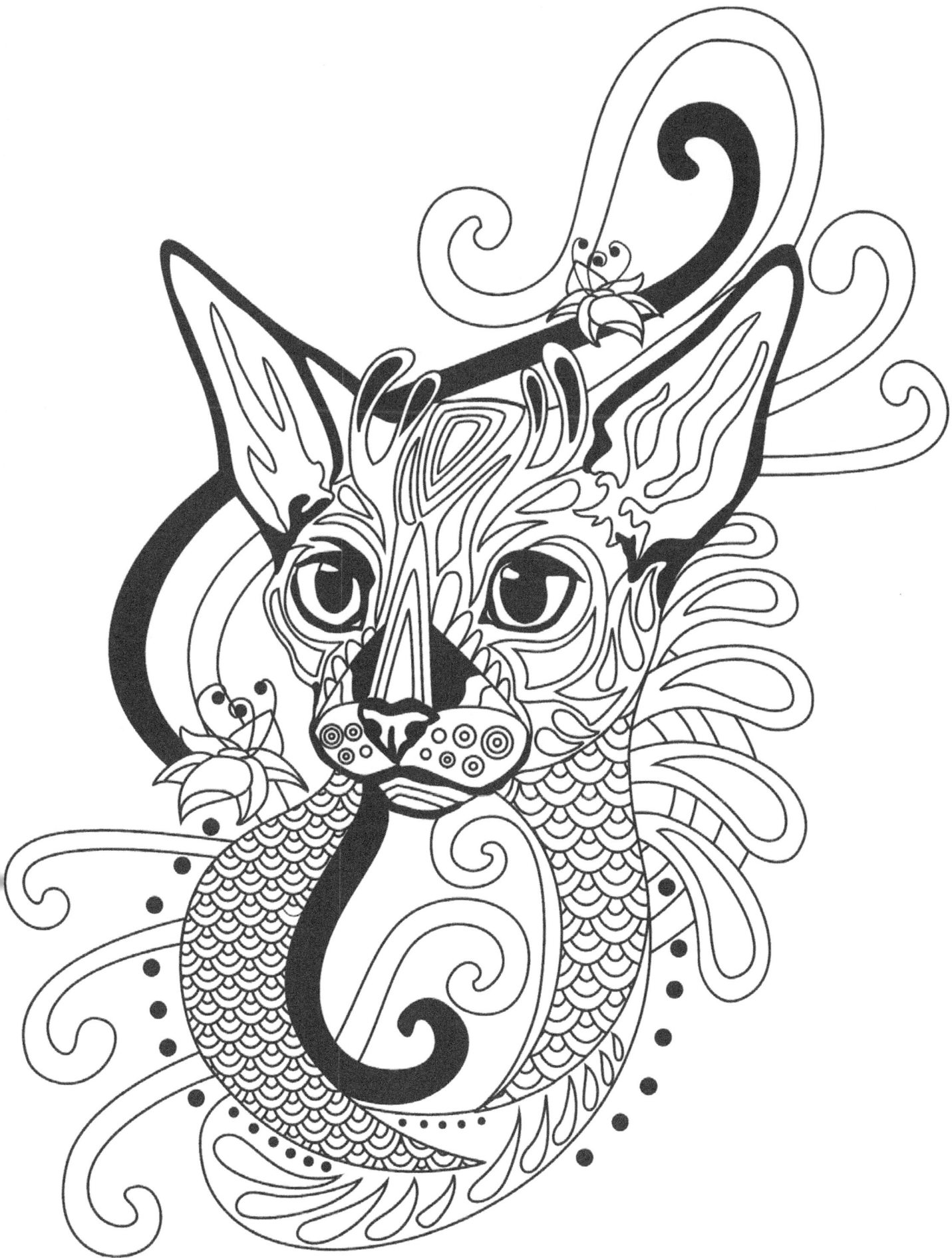

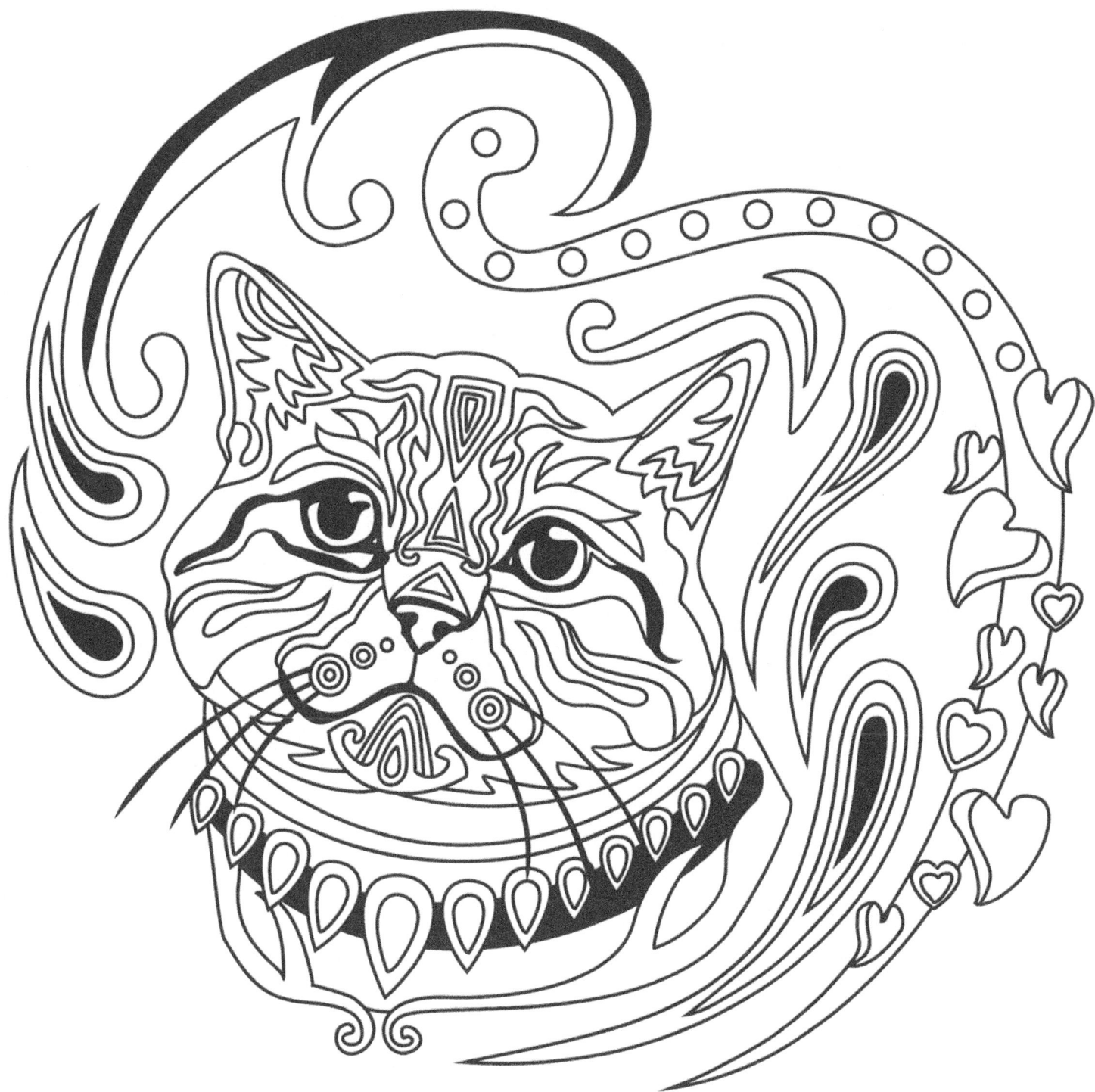

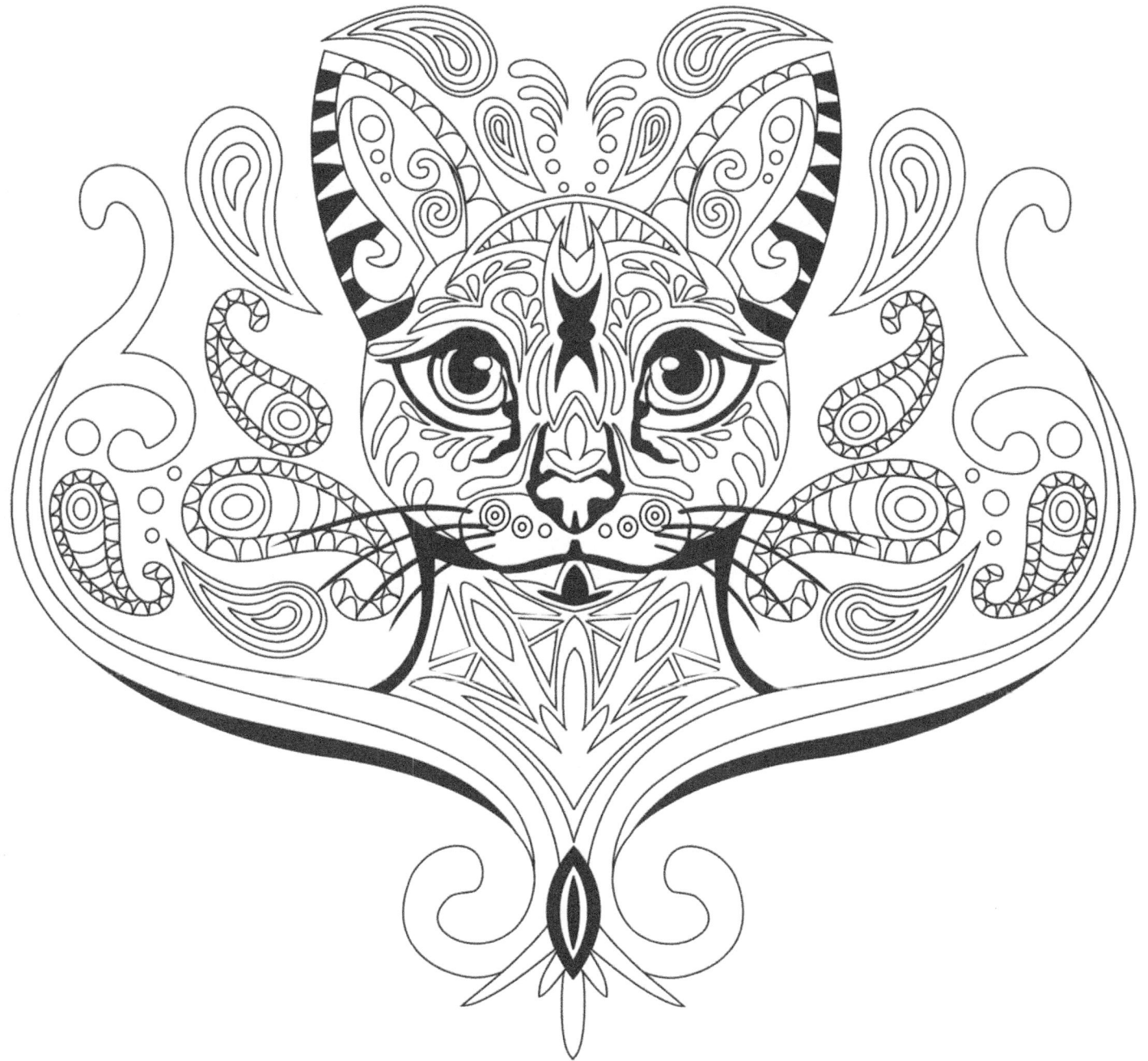

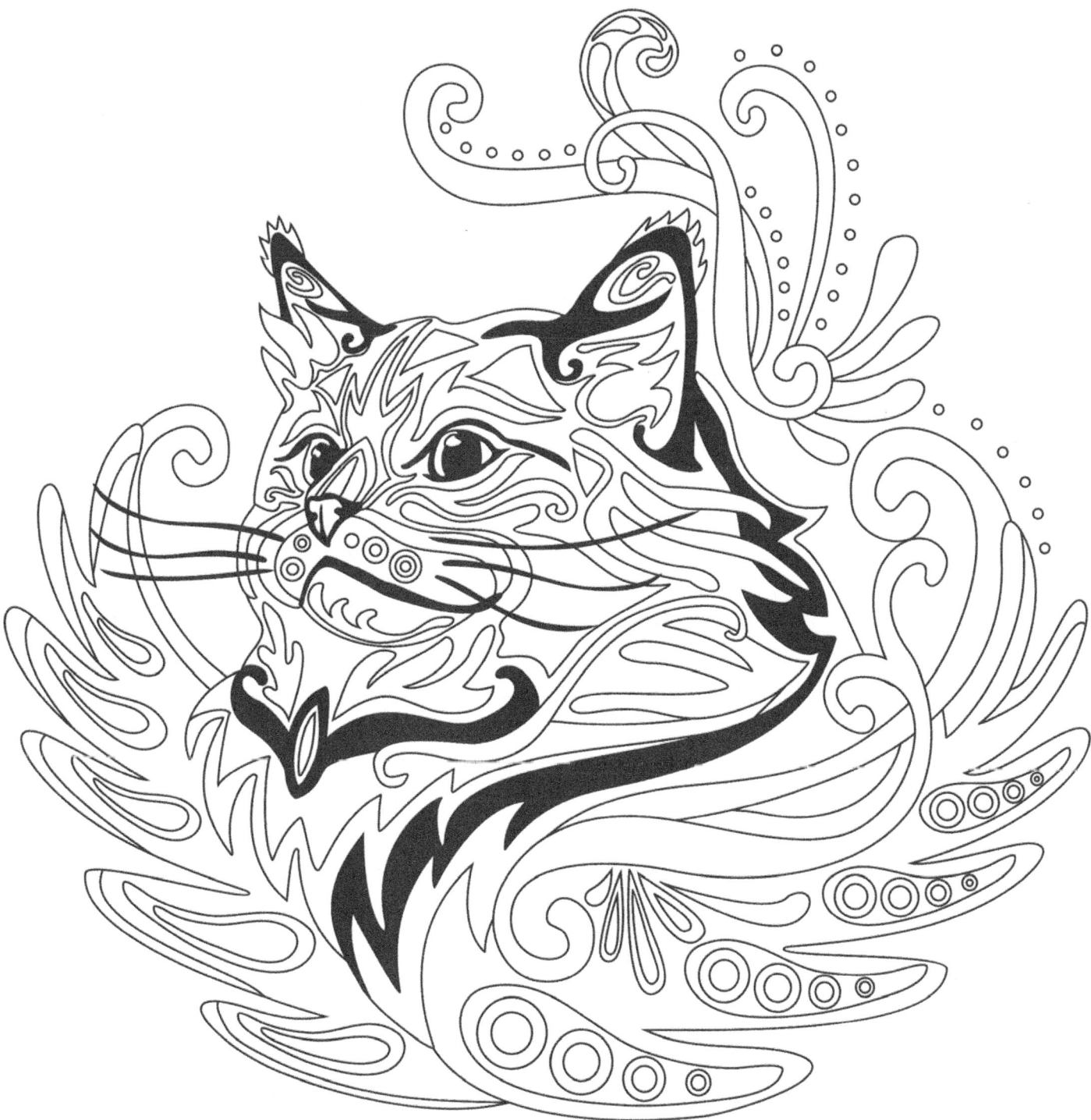

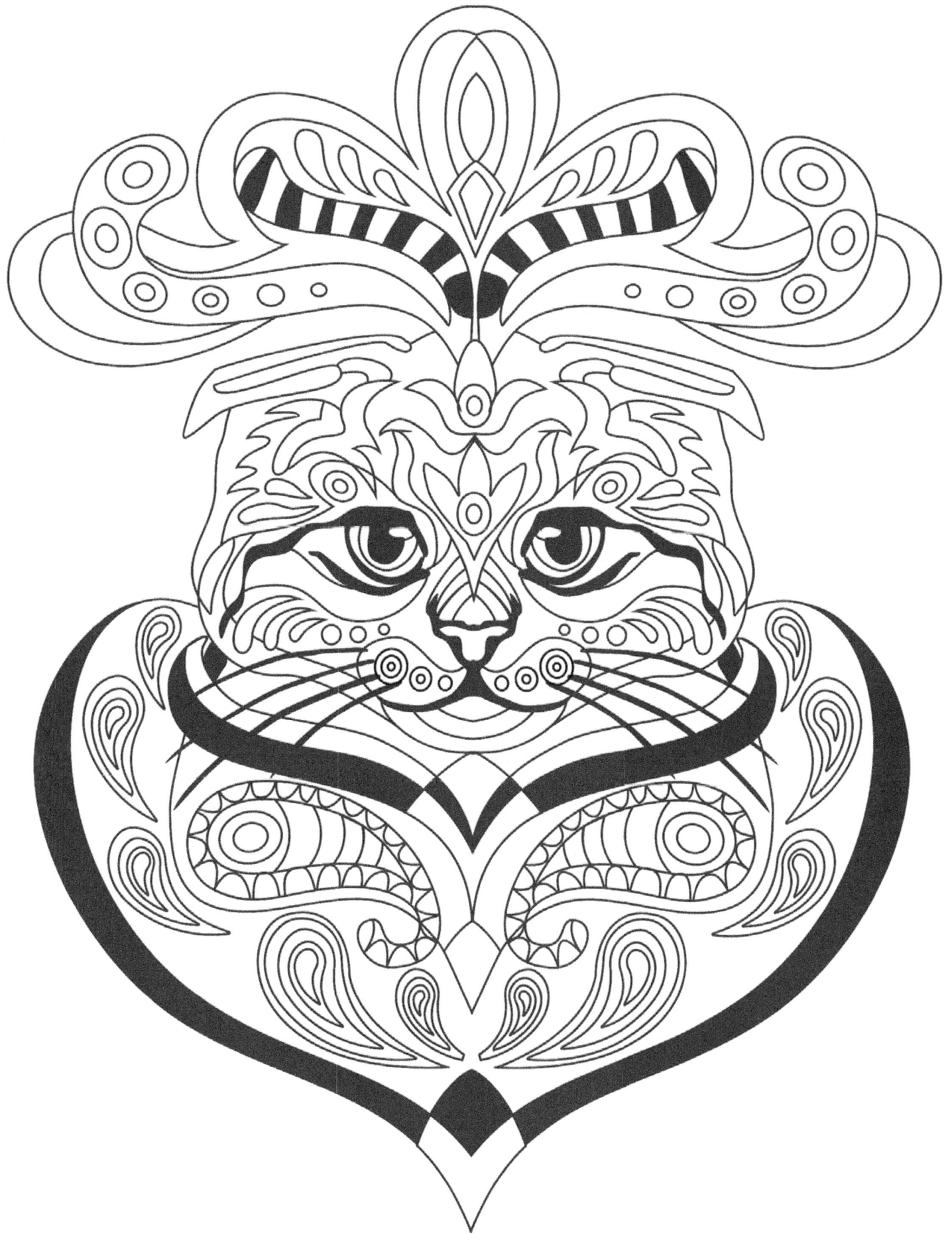

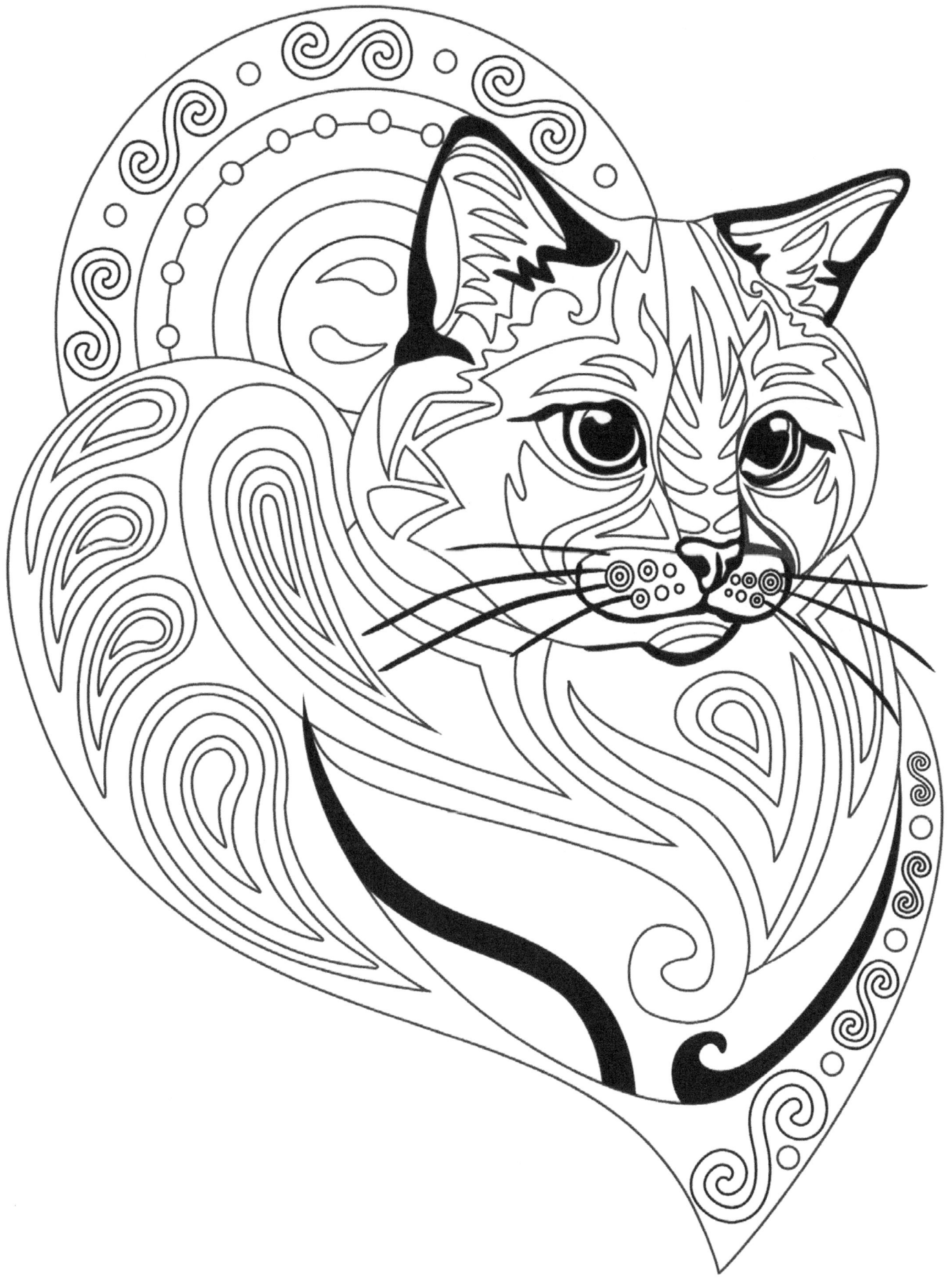

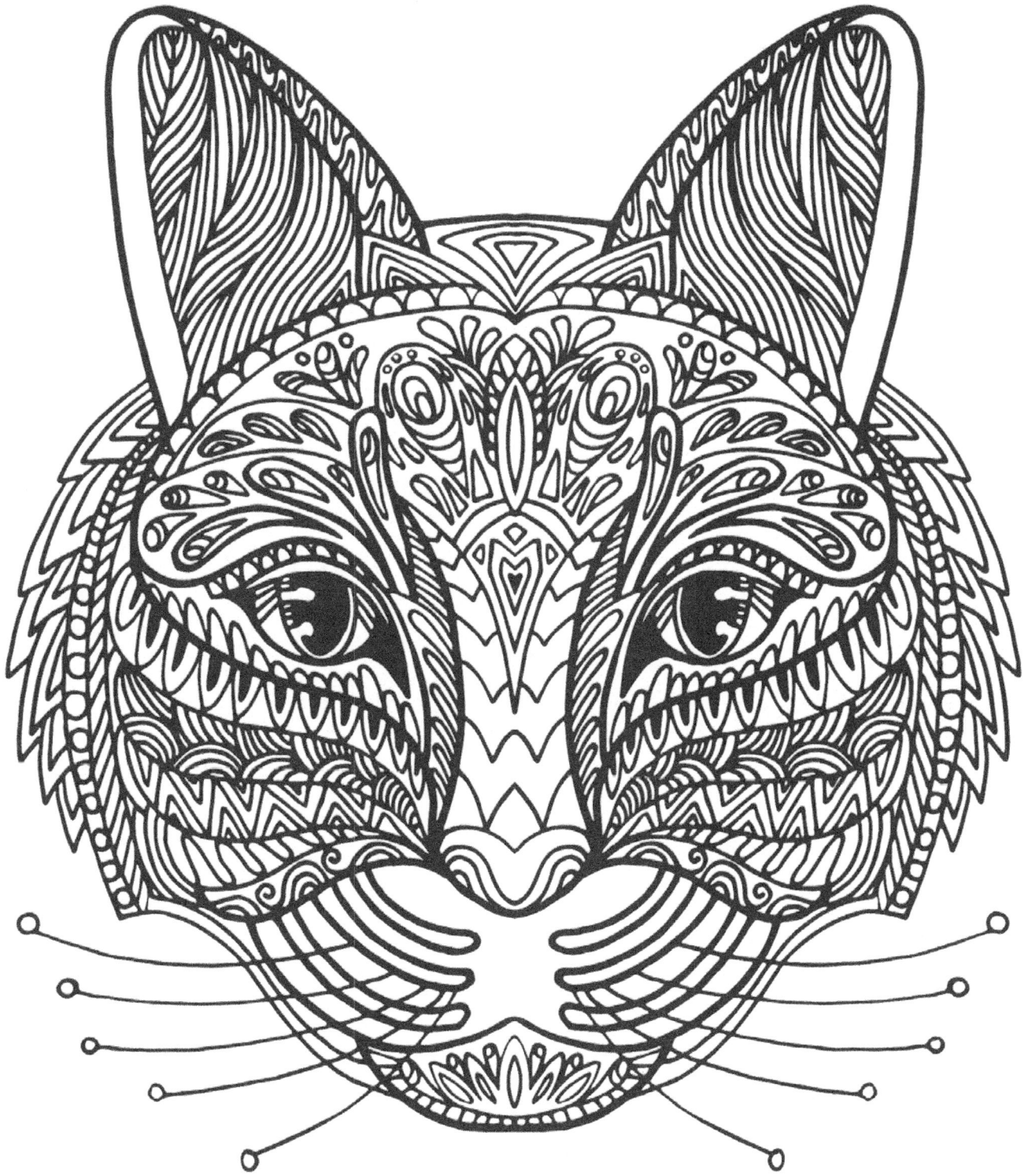

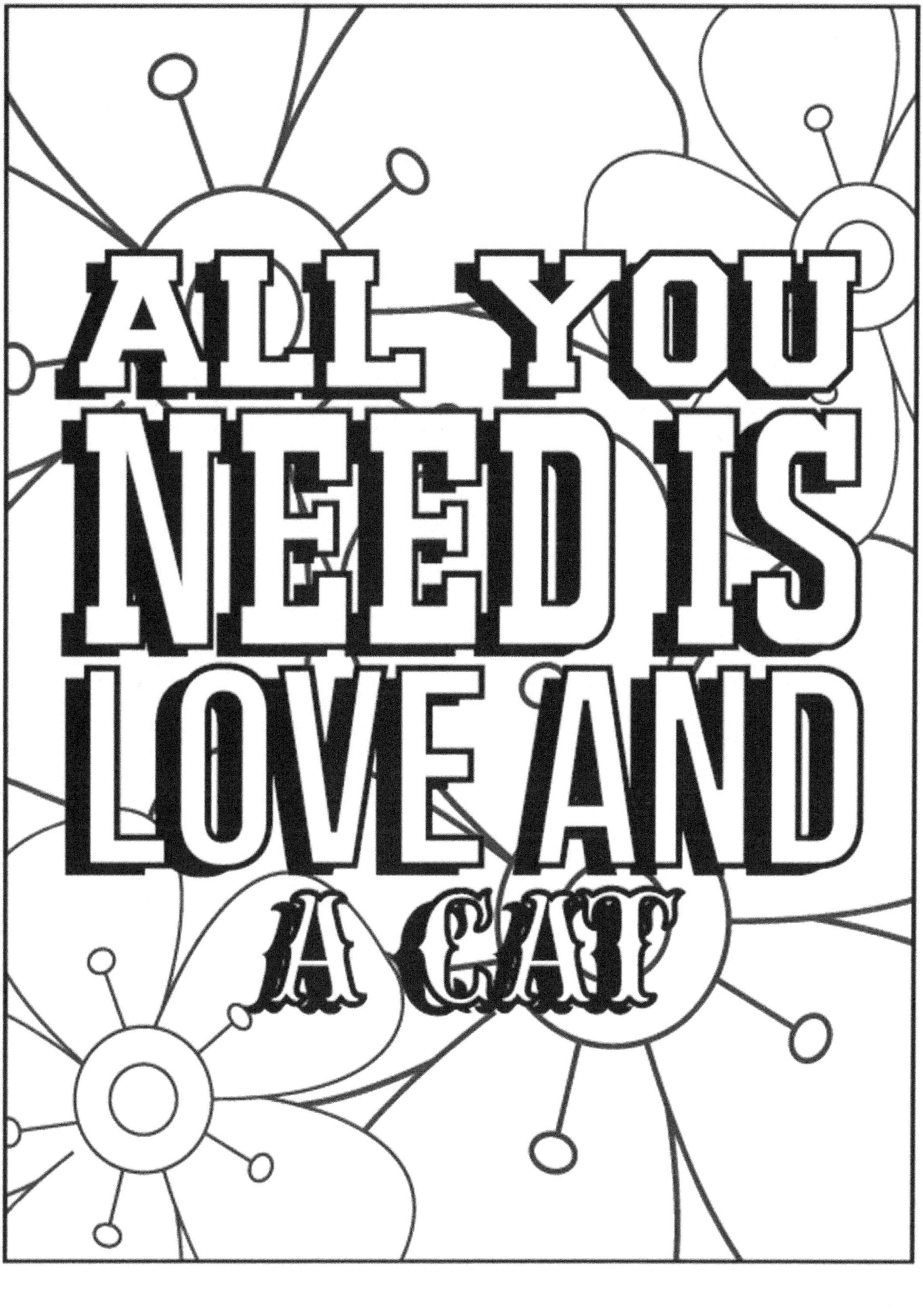
ALL YOU
NEED IS
LOVE AND
A CAT

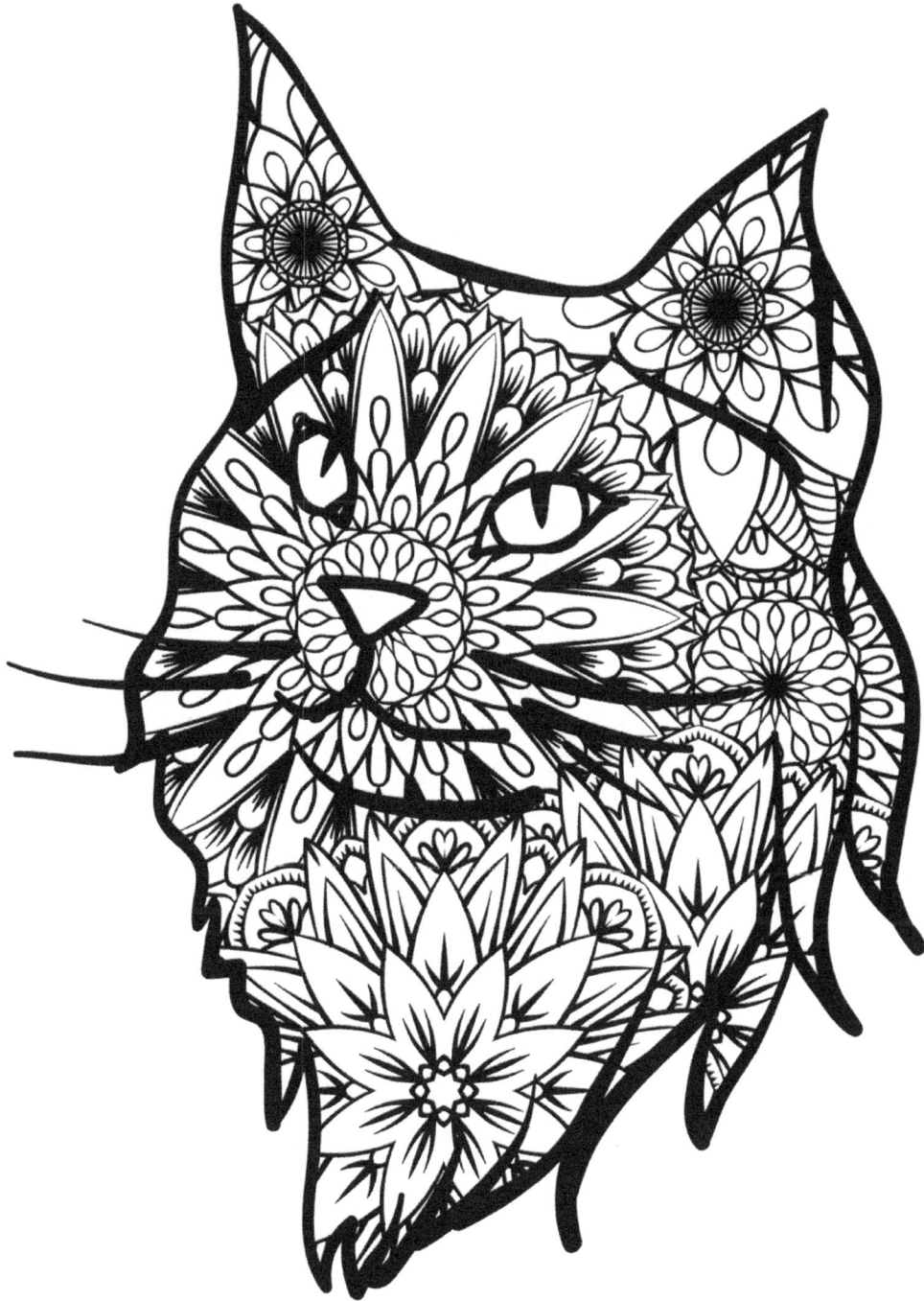

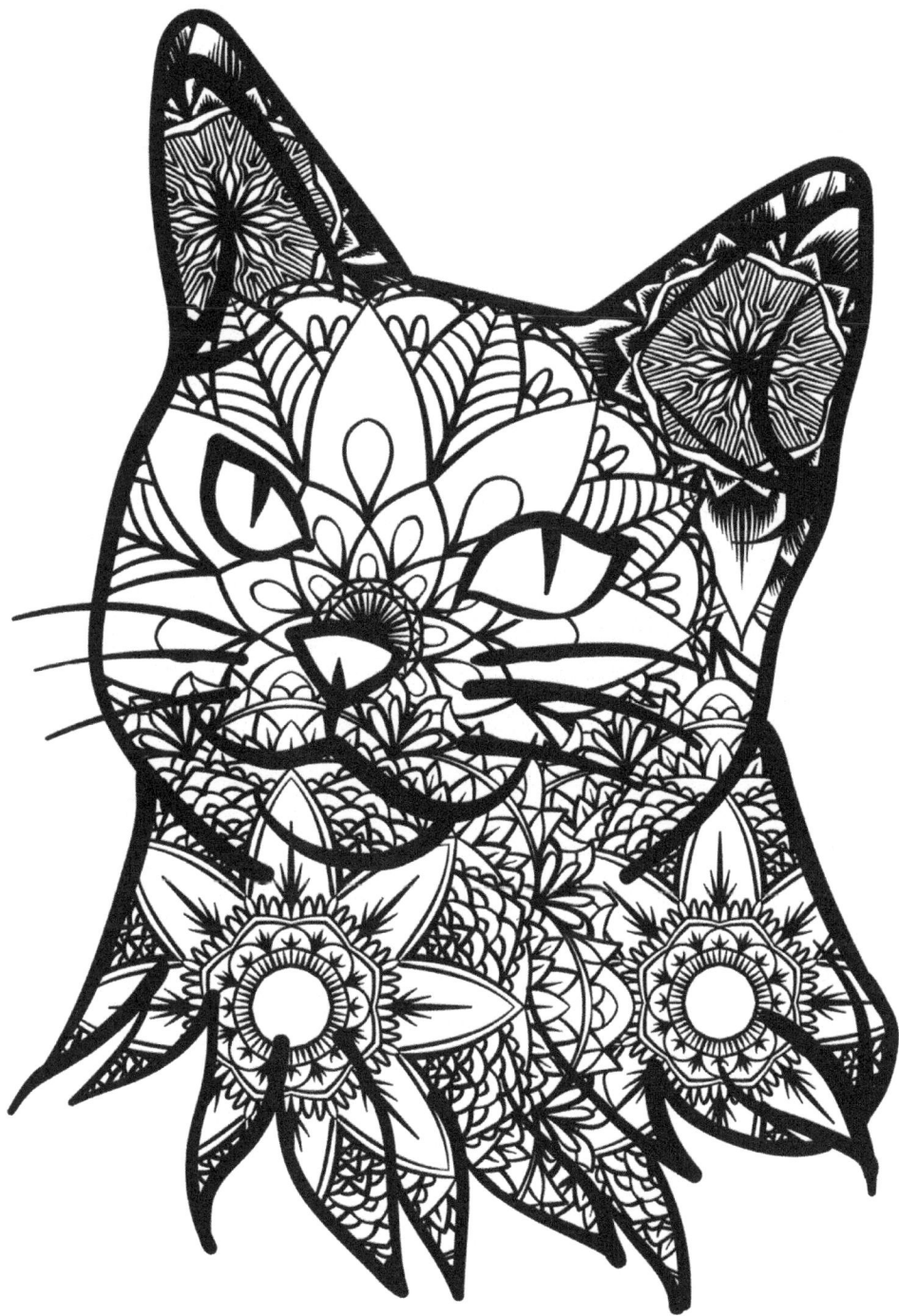

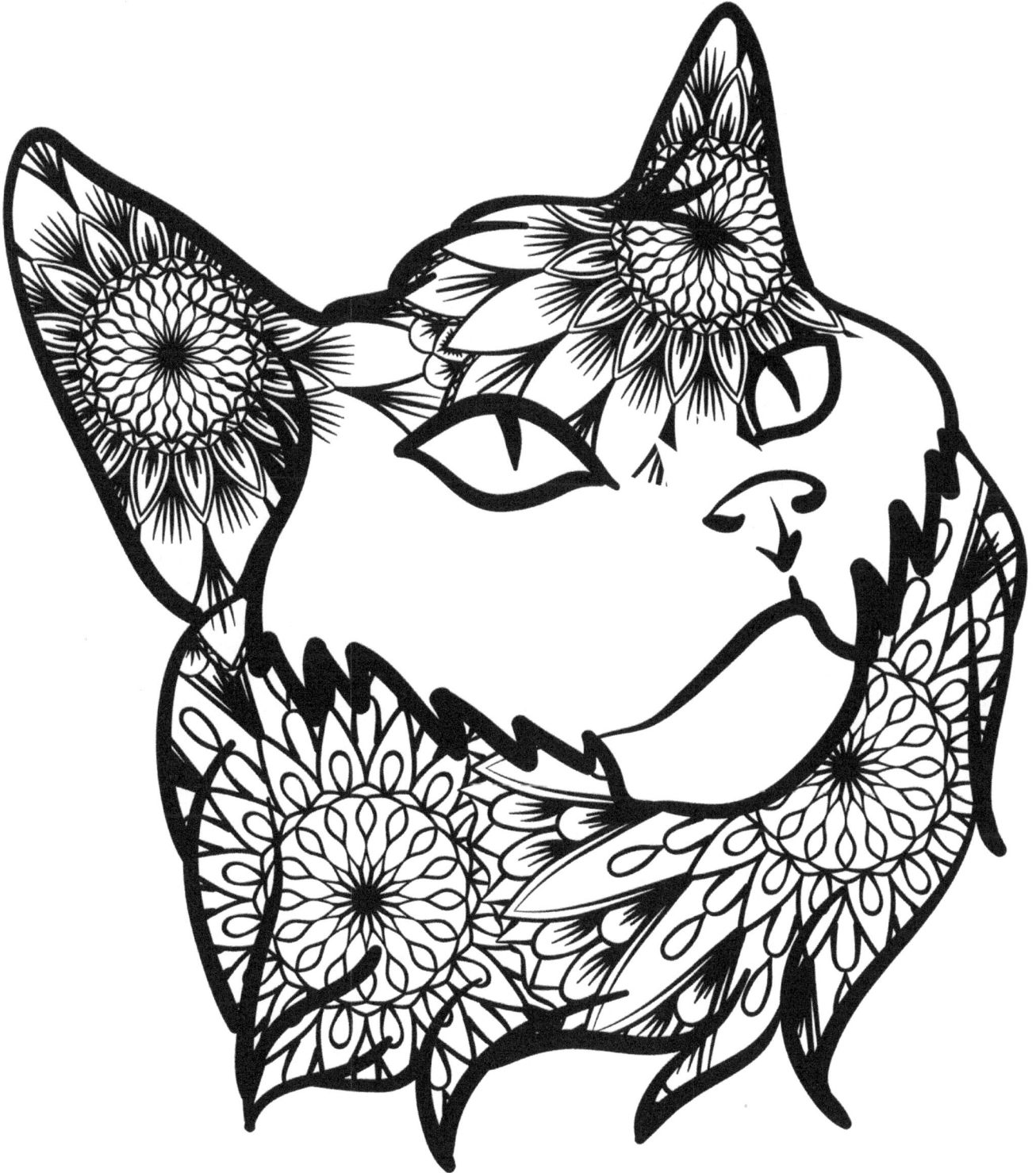

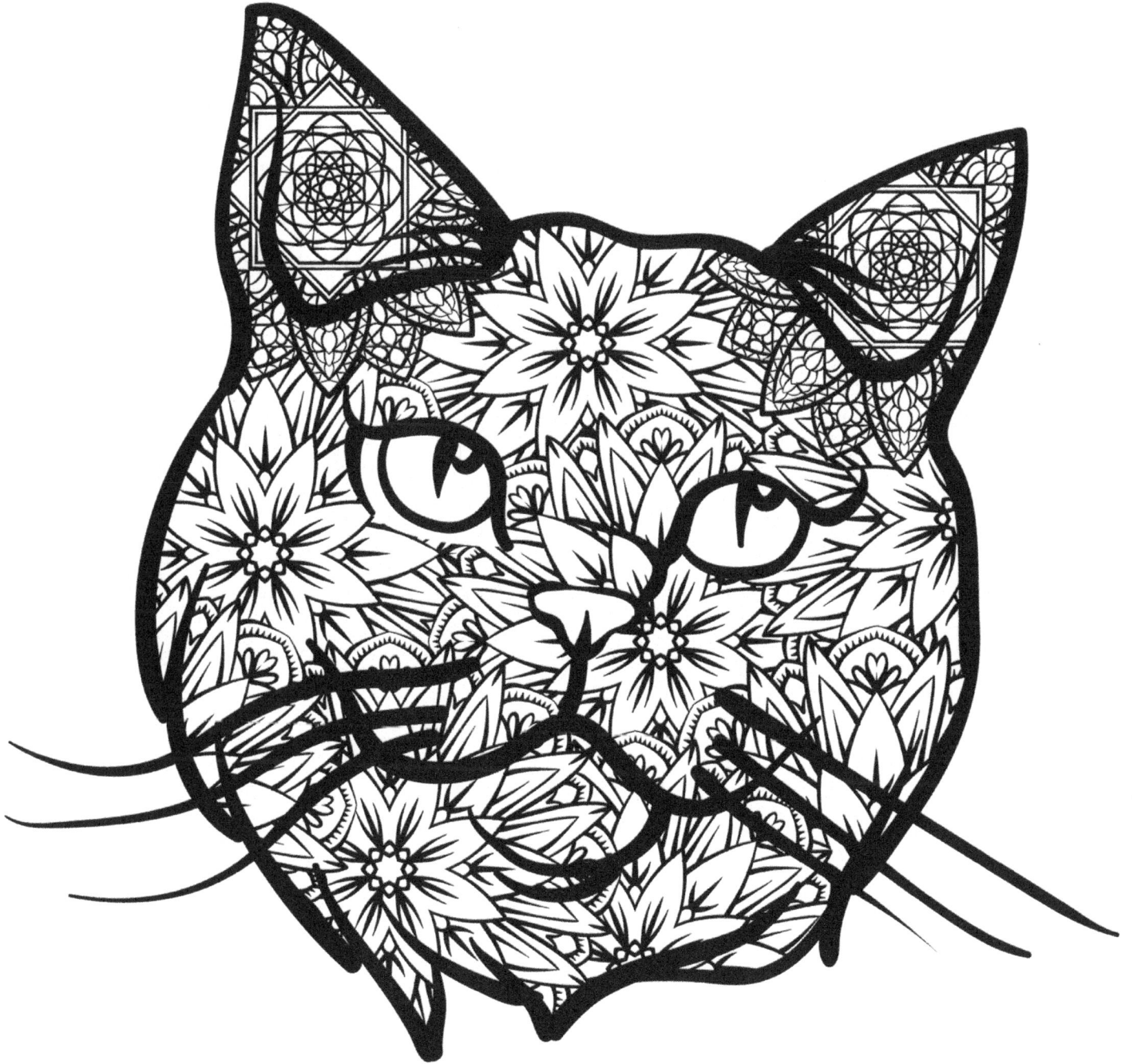

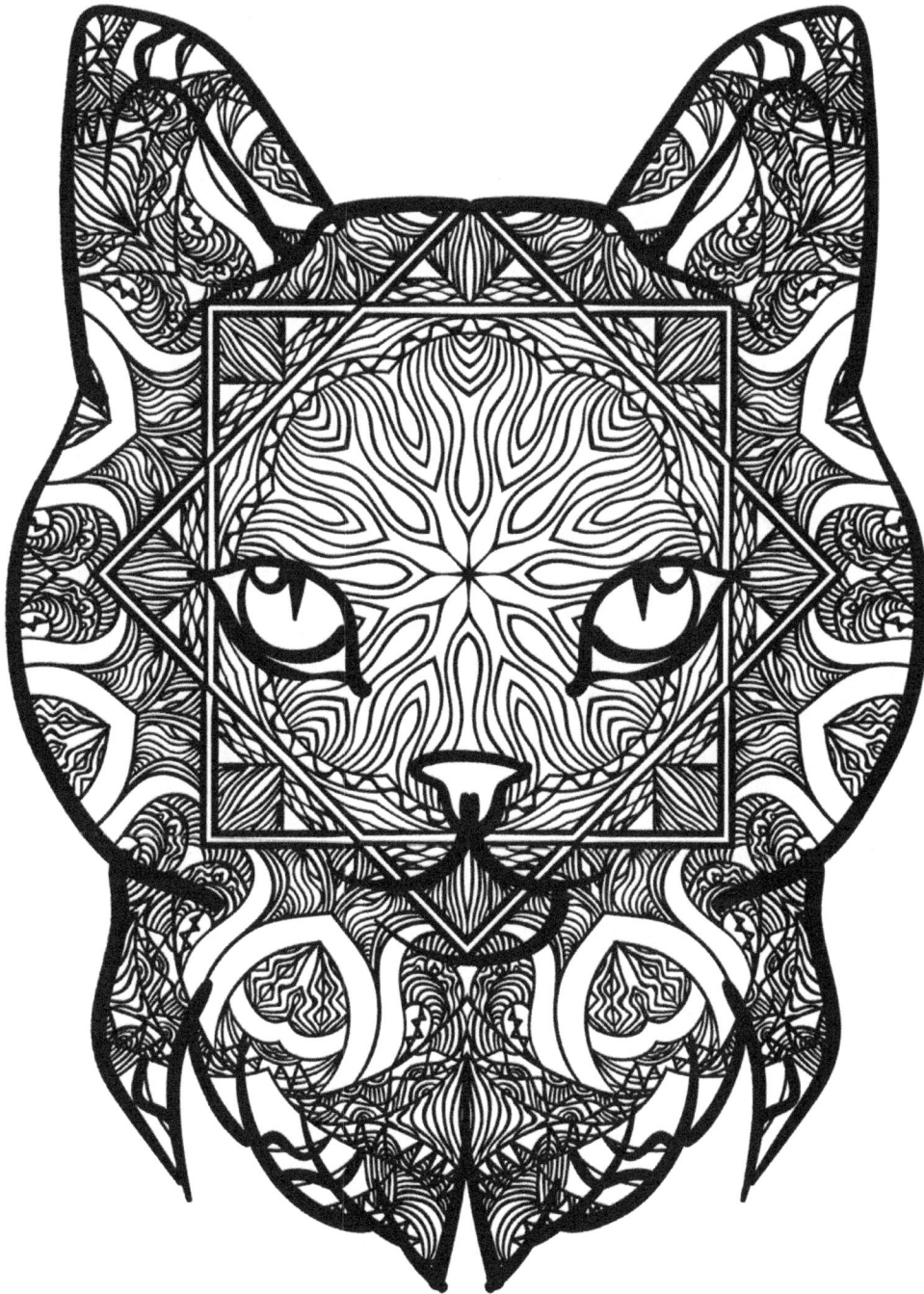

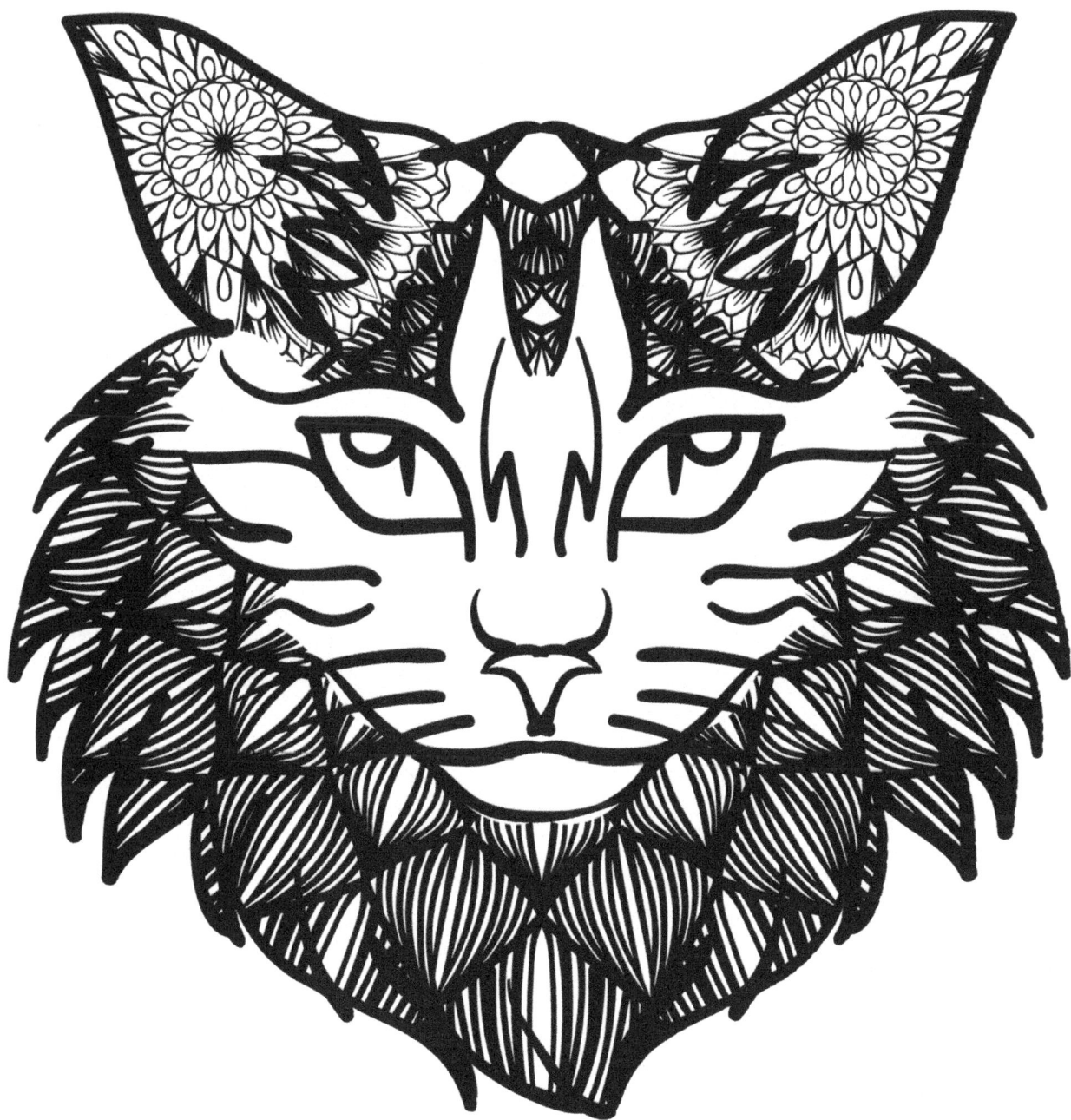

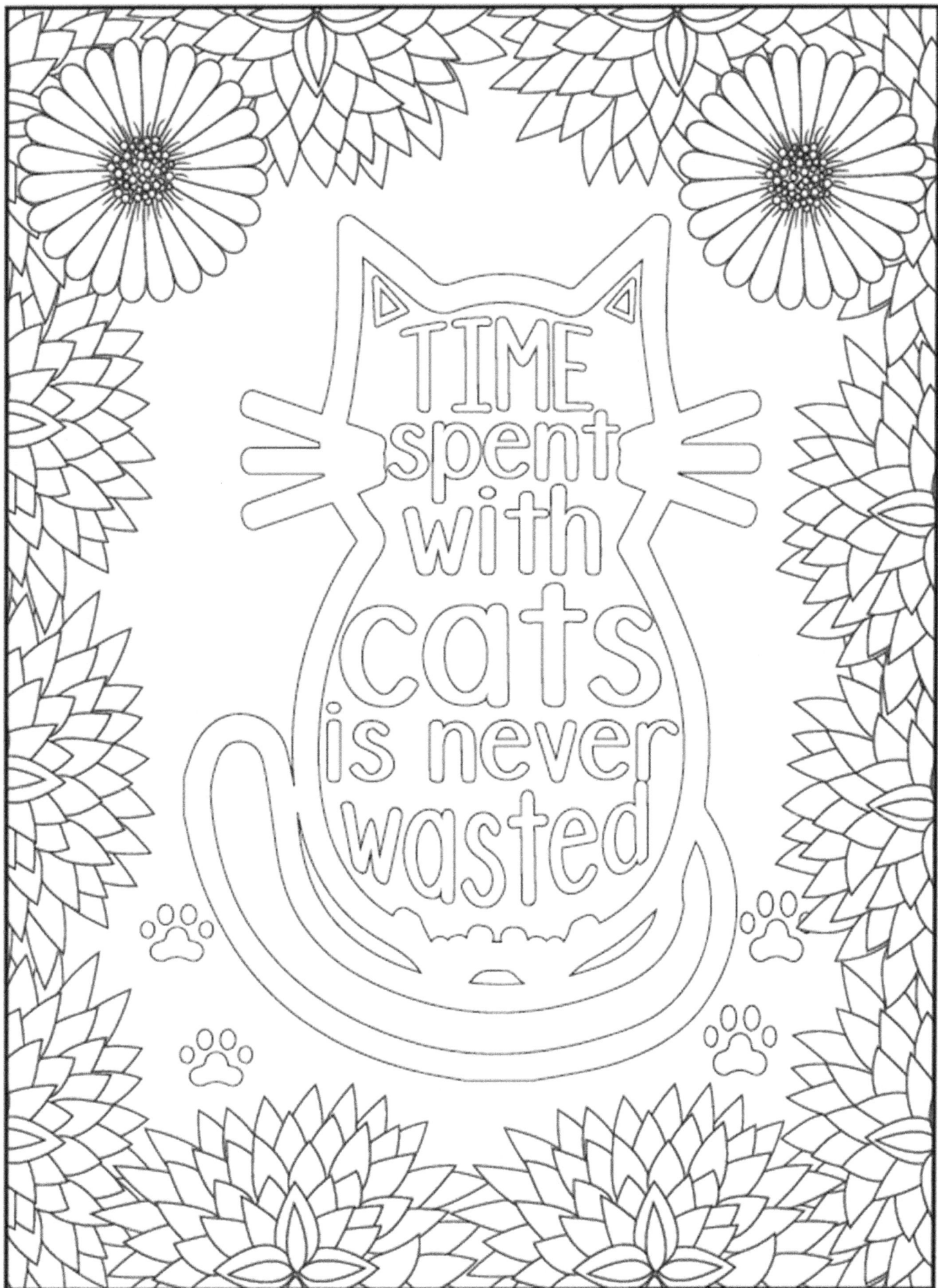

TIME spent with cats is never wasted

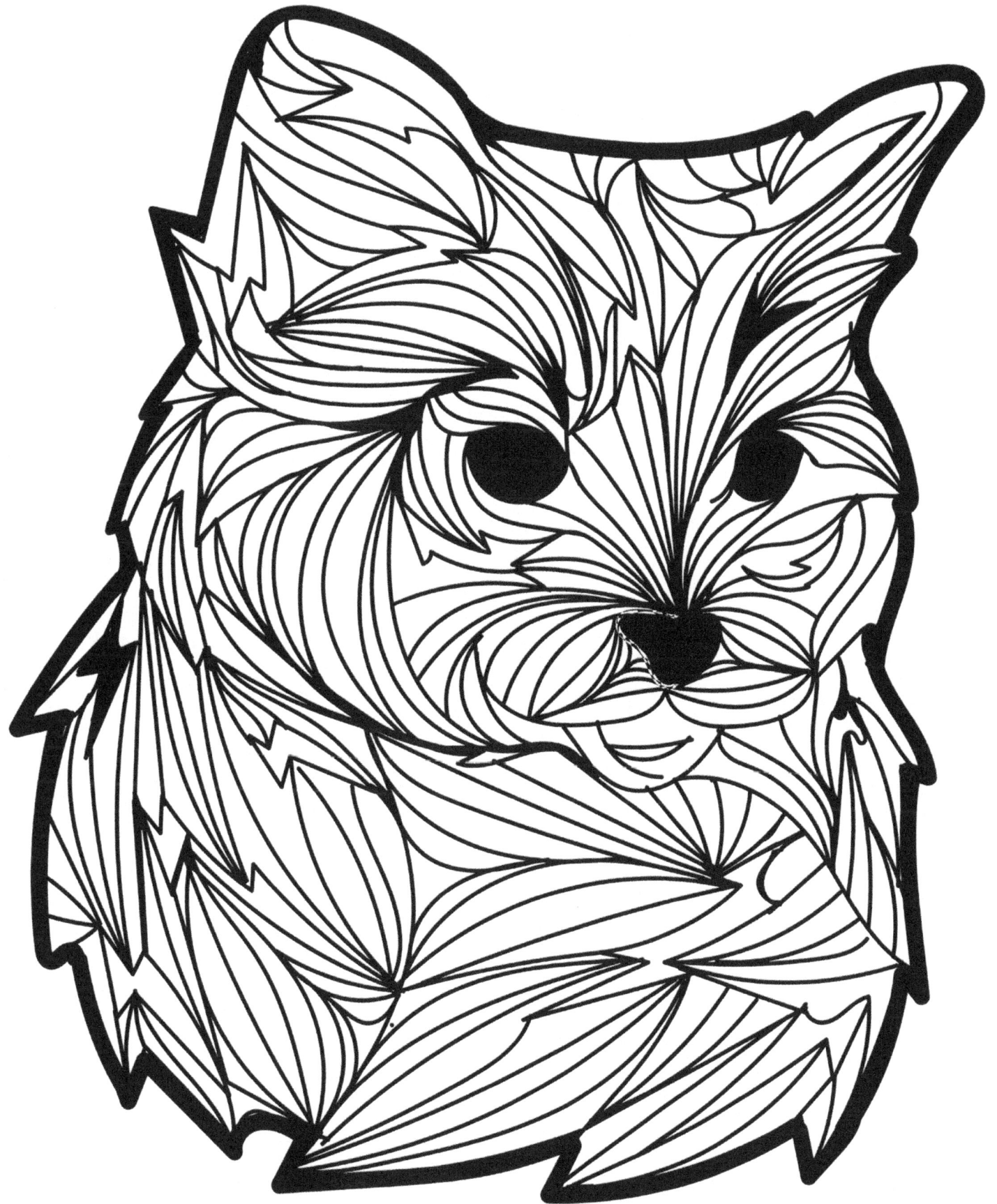

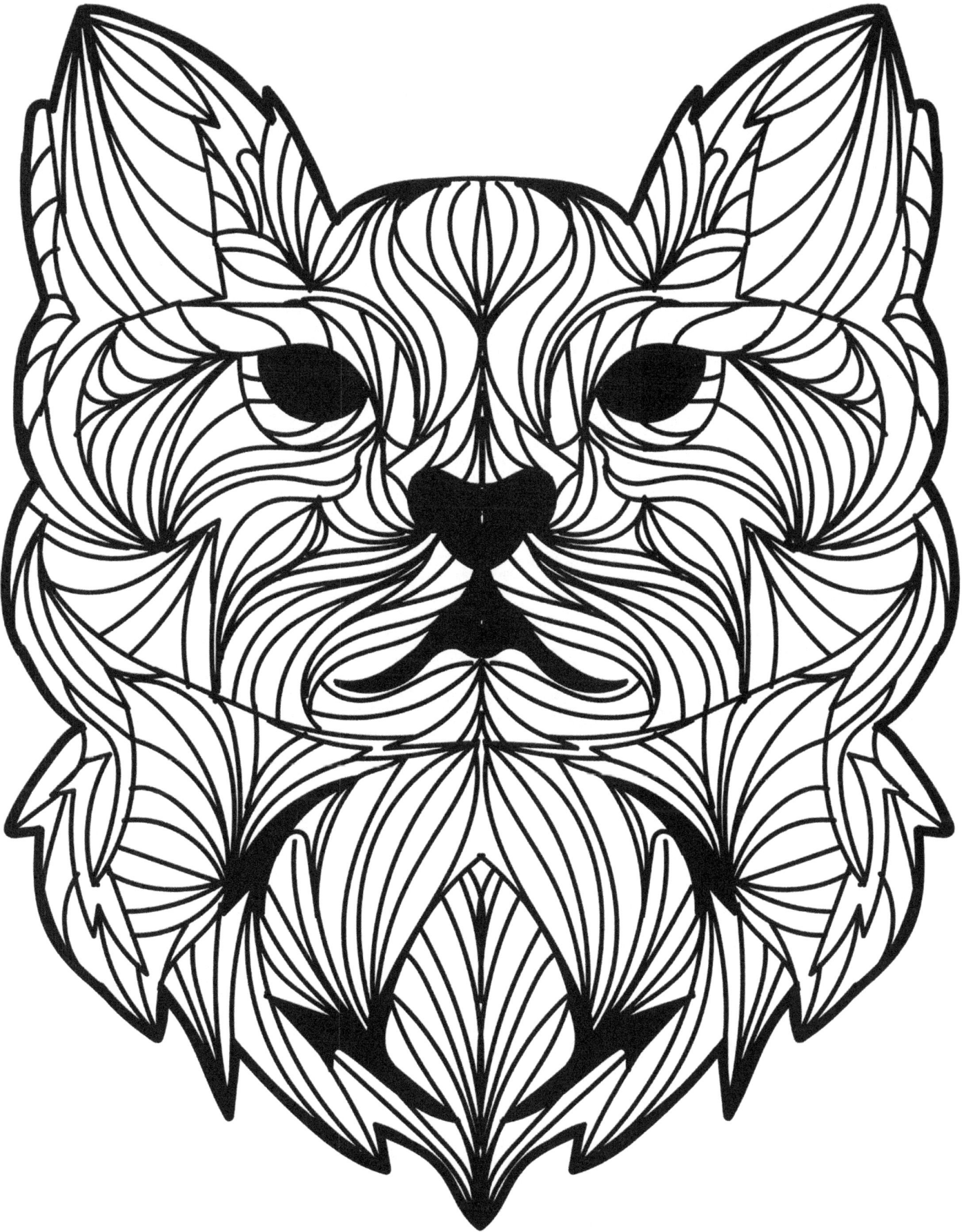

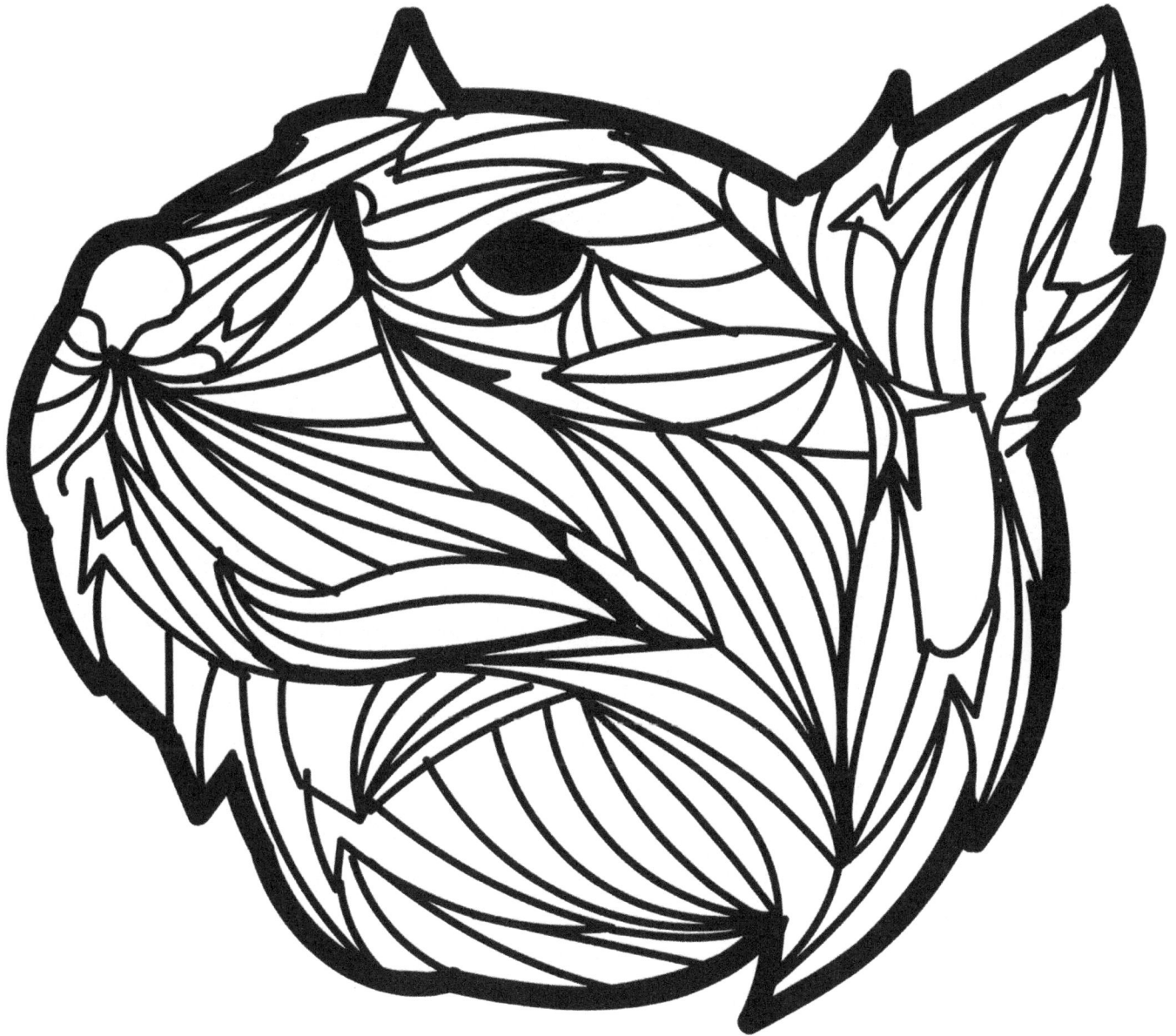

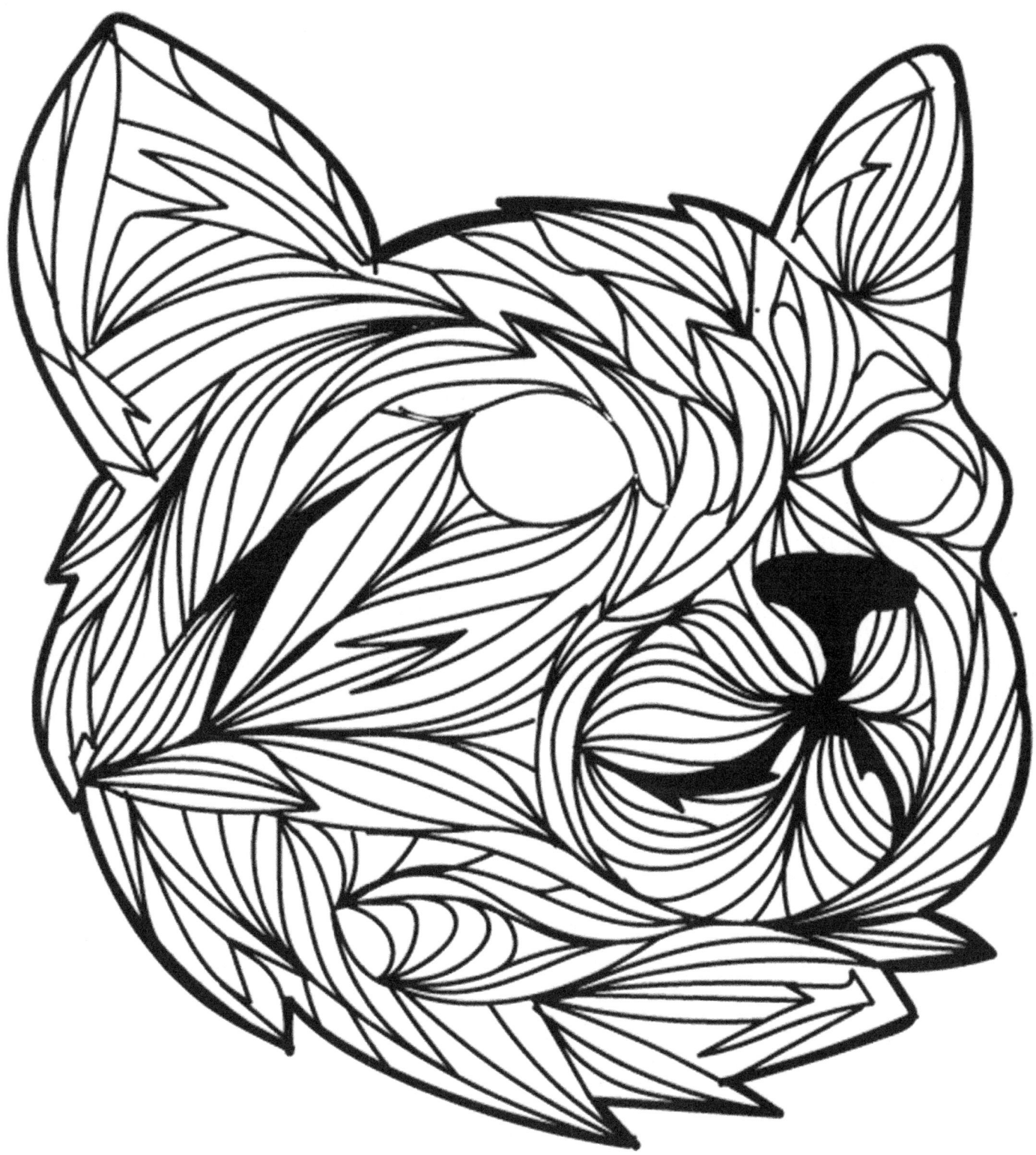

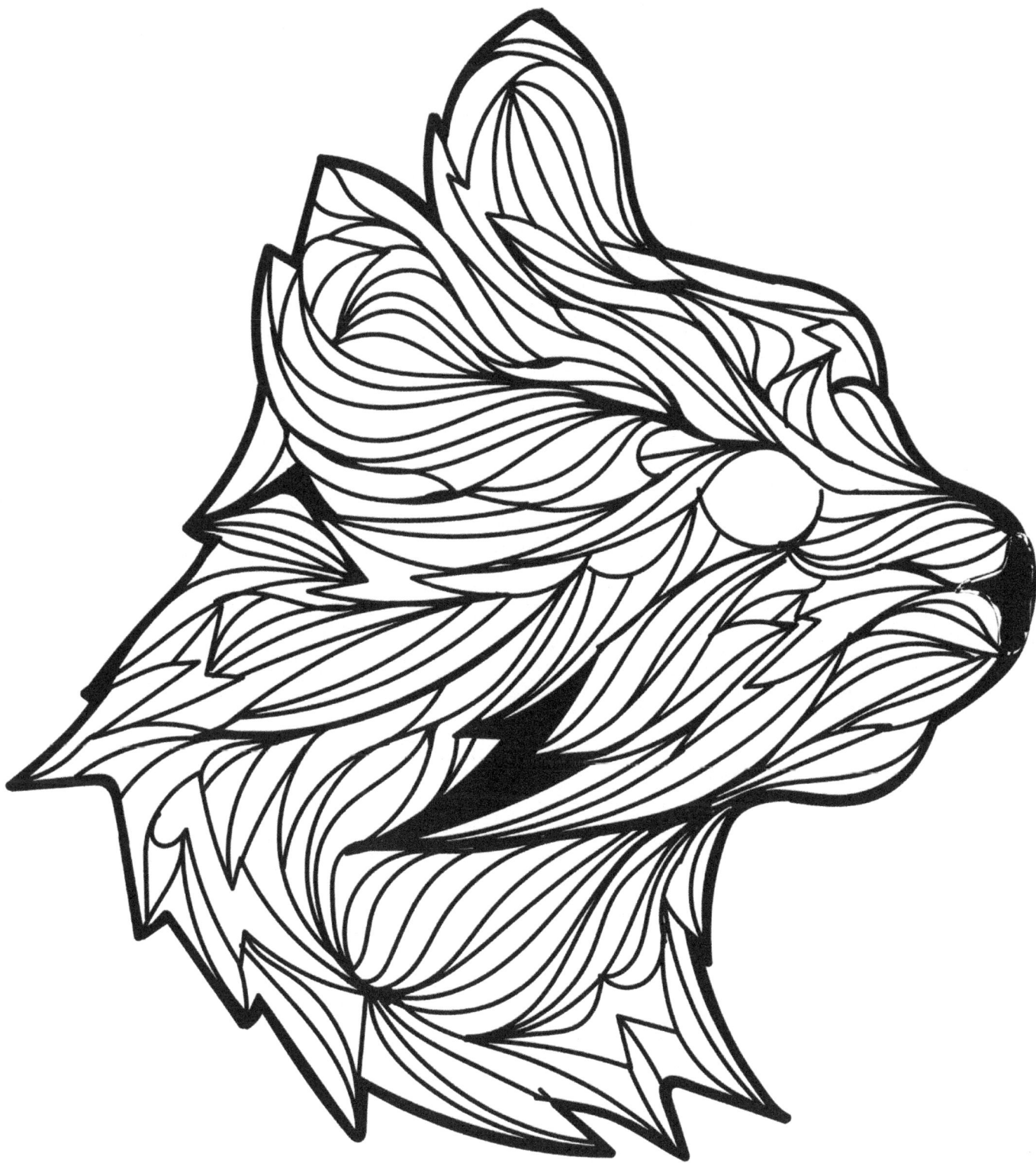

People who love

cats

have some of

the biggest

hearts around

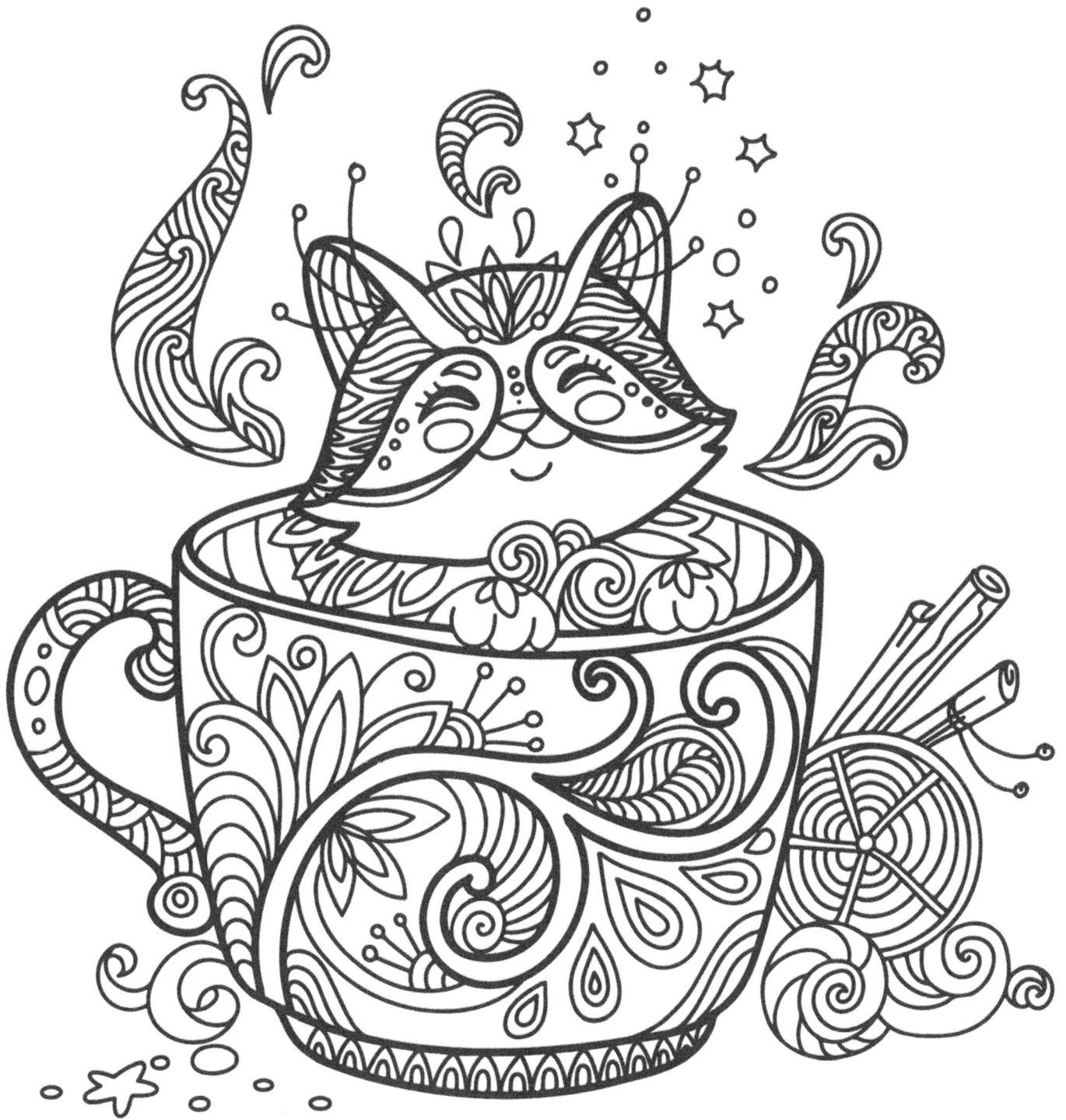

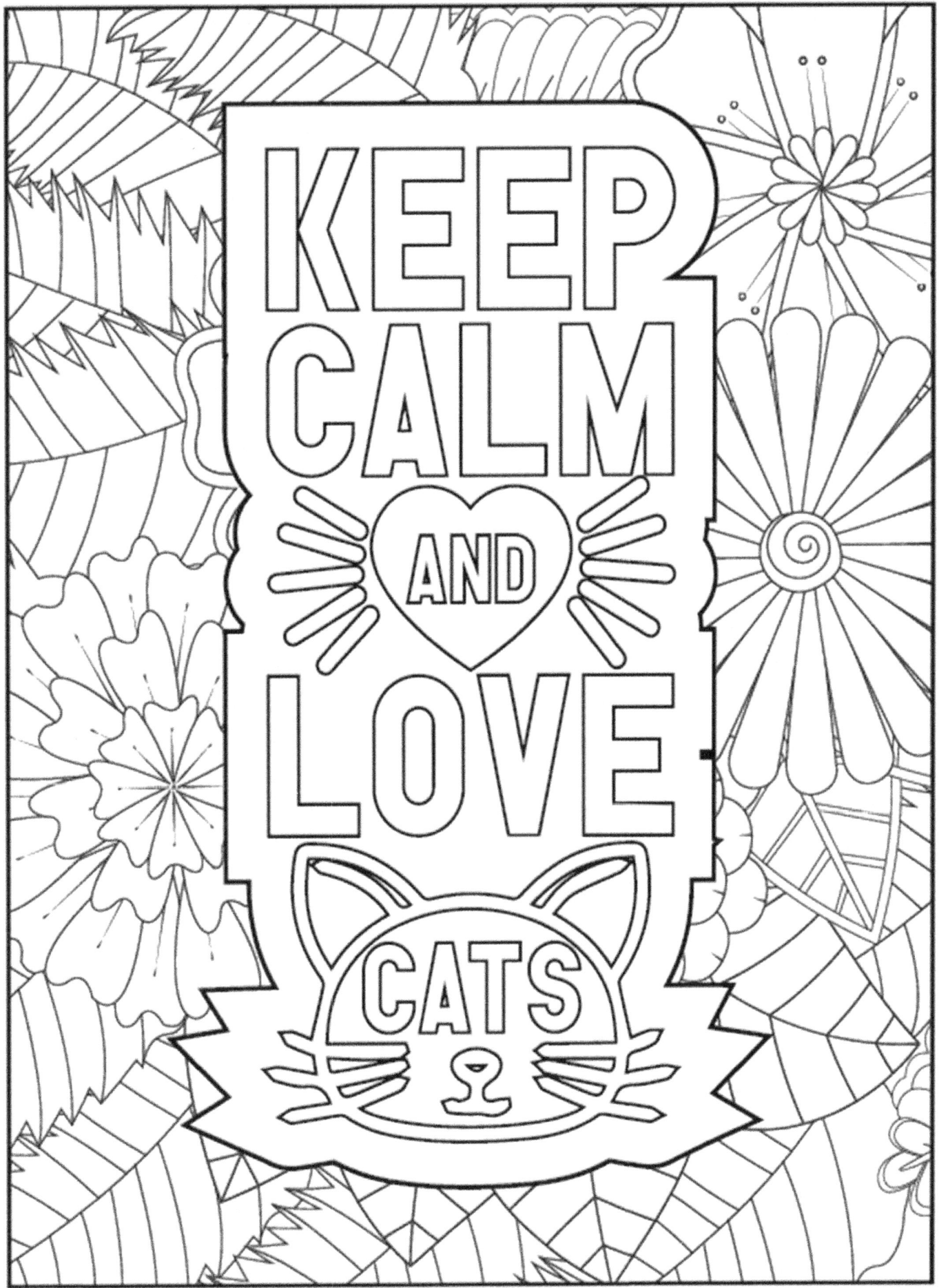

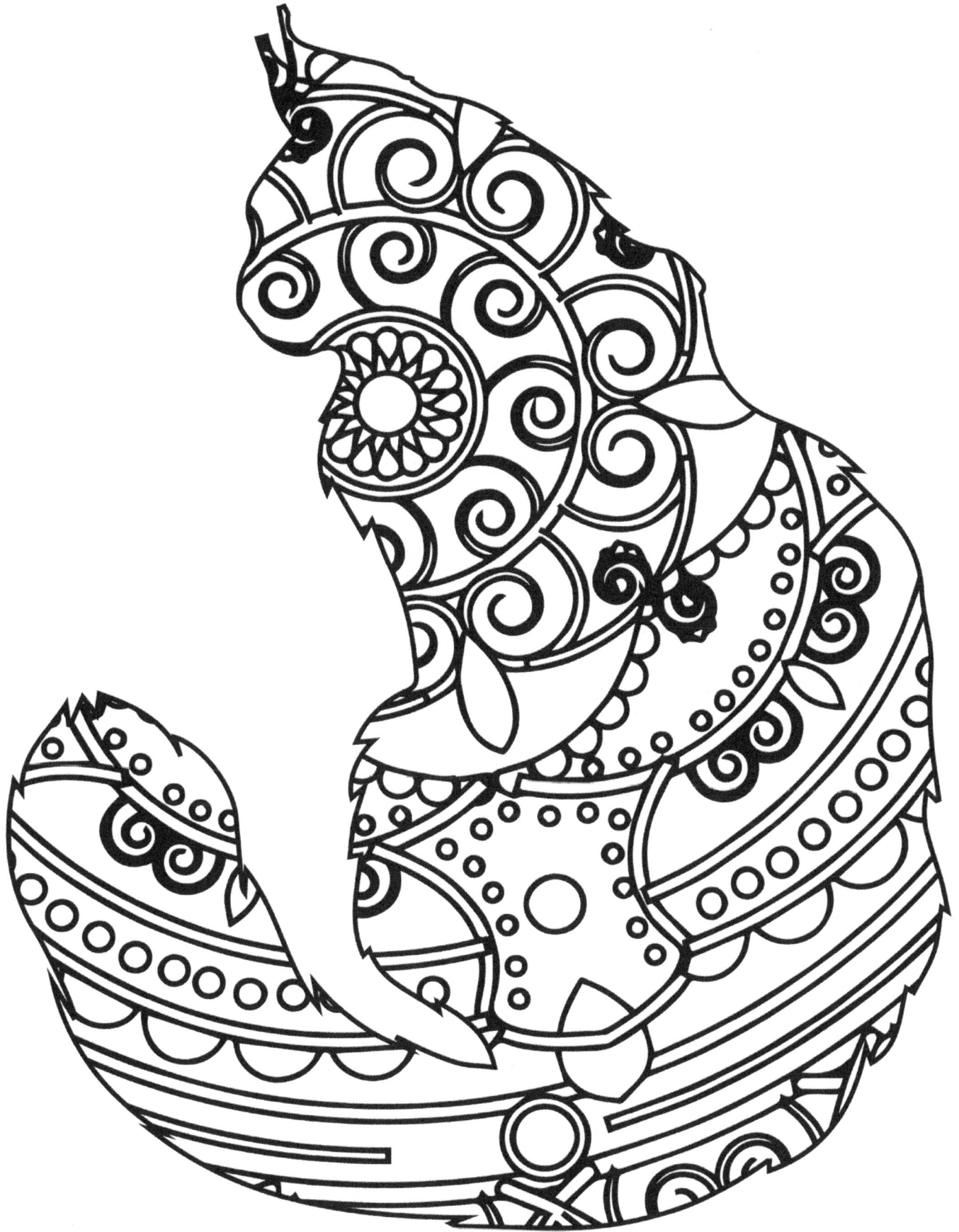

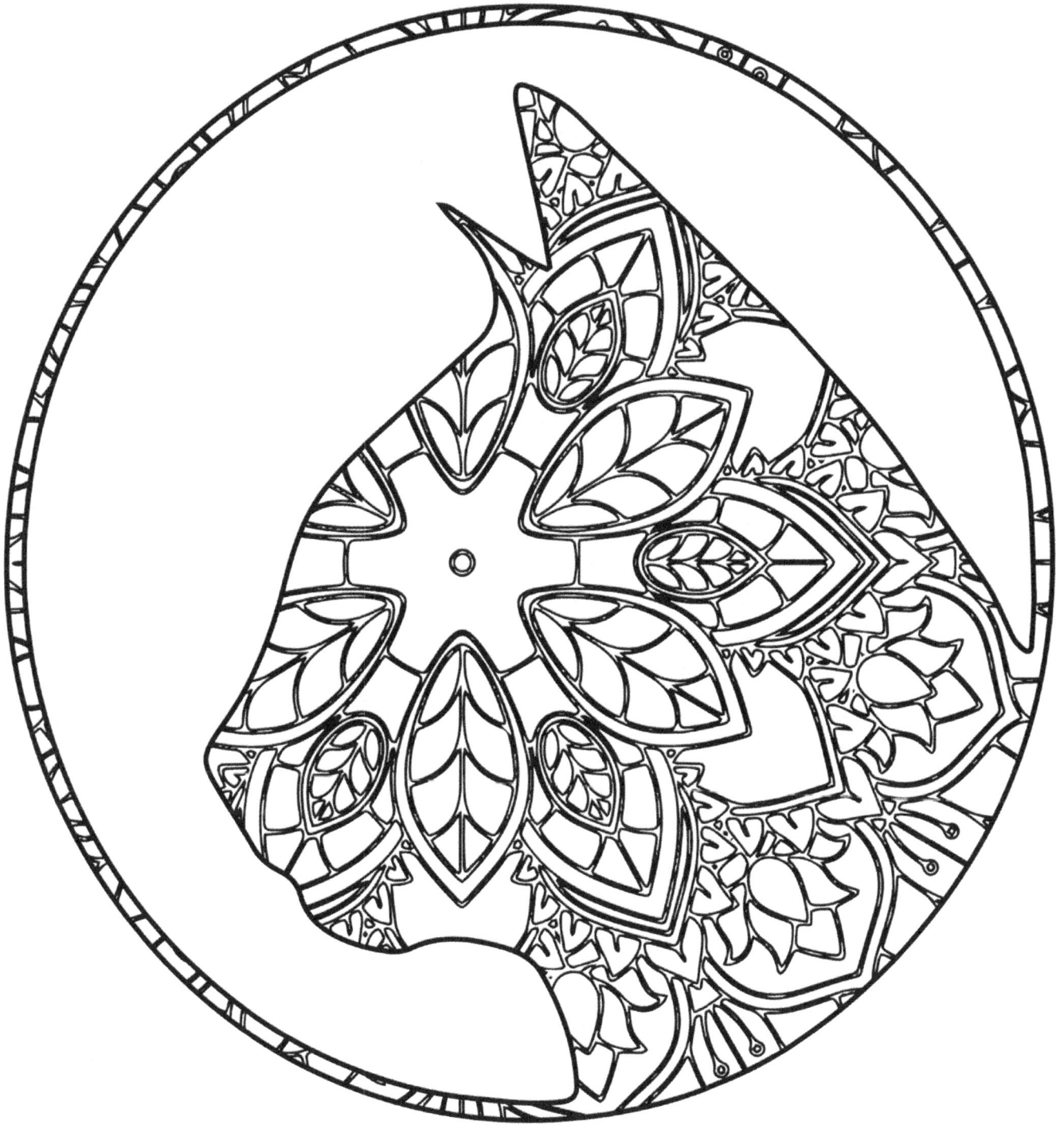

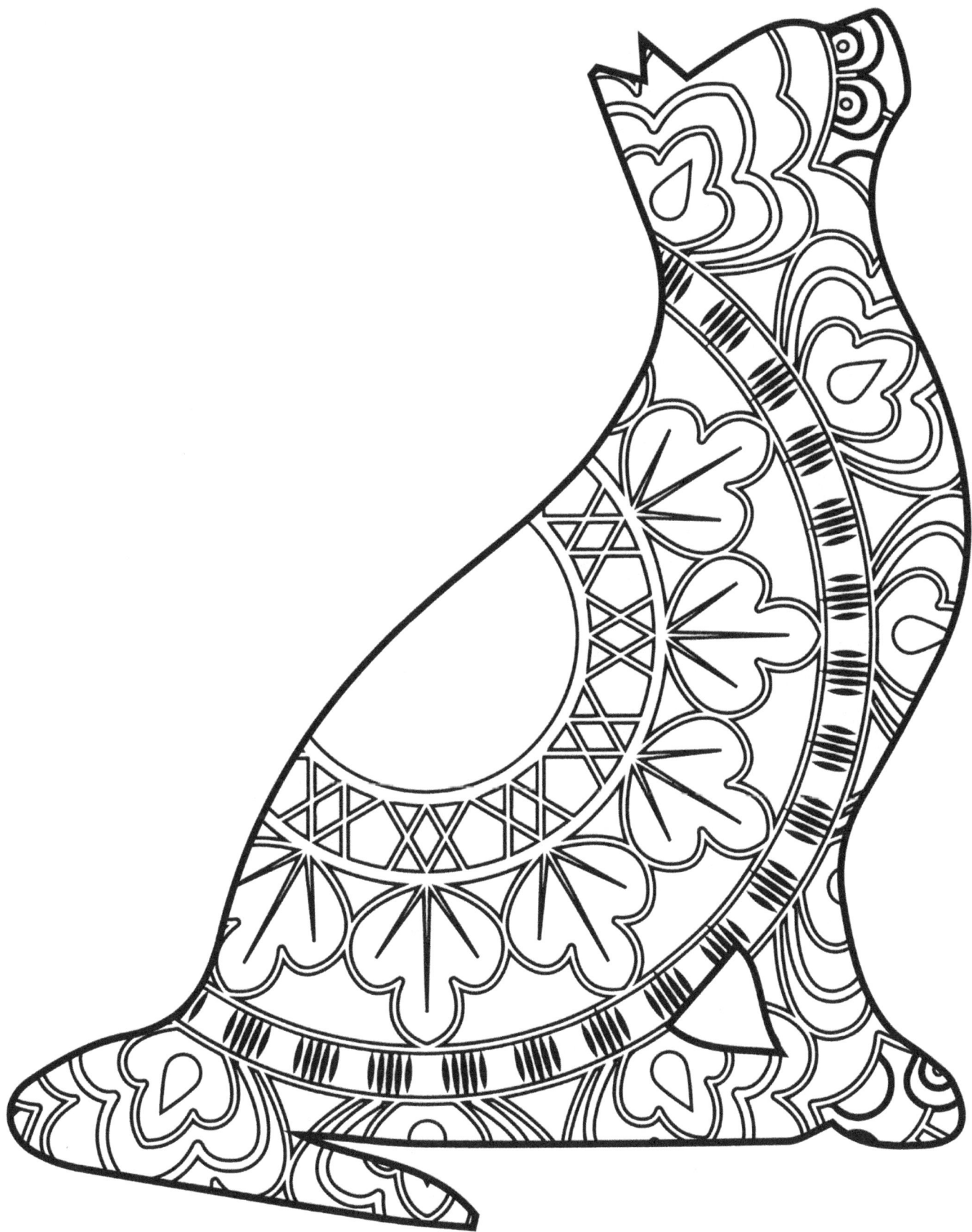

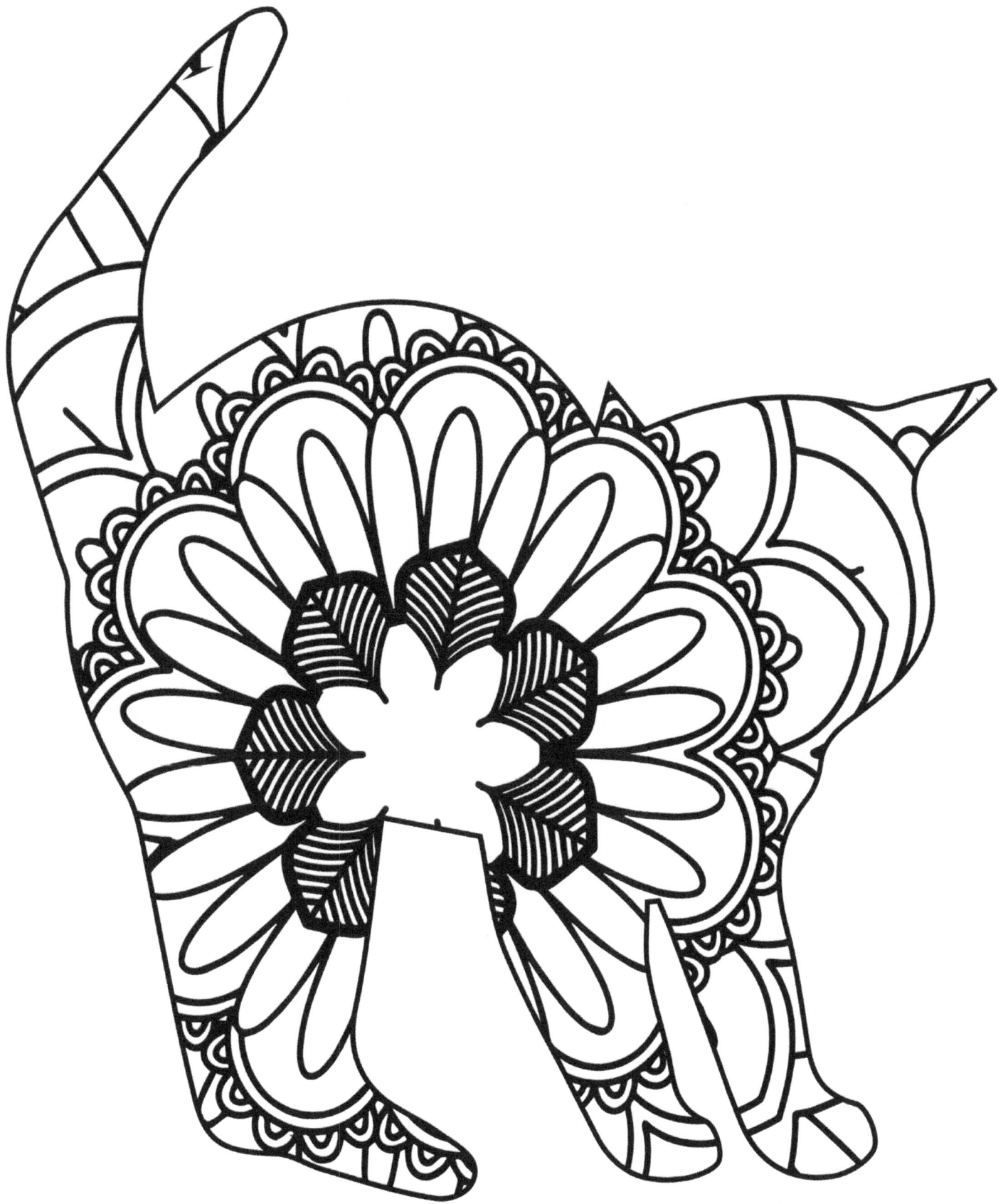

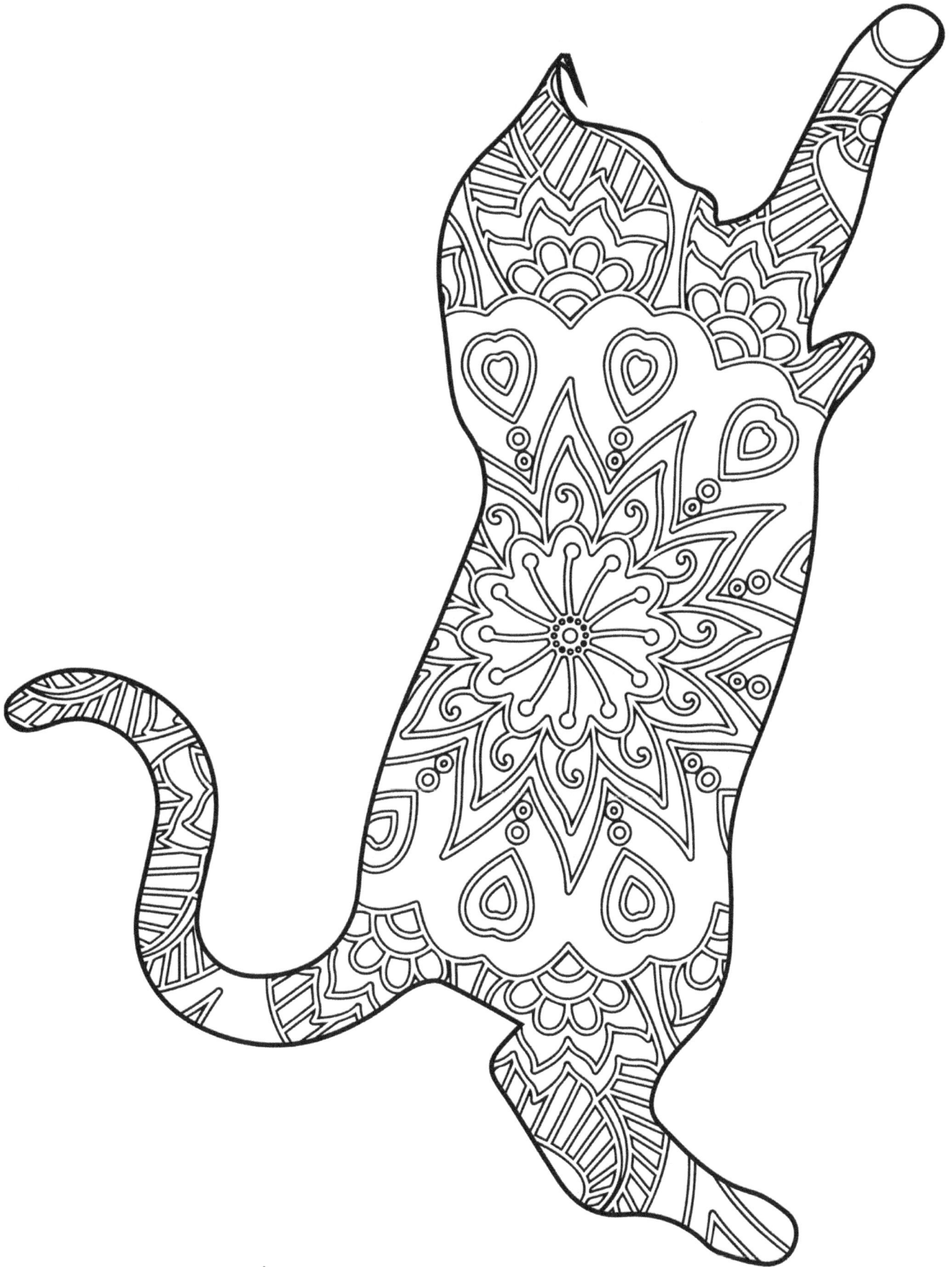

Made in the USA
Coppell, TX
20 March 2022